Living

on

the Bright Side!

by
Cindy Schaap

Living *on* the Bright Side!

Principles for Lasting Joy, Especially for Ladies

Christian Womanhood / Crown Point, Indiana
Mrs. Cindy Schaap, Senior Editor
Mr. Dan Wolfe, Managing Editor

ISBN: 0-9719019-7-X

All Scriptures used in this volume
are from the King James Bible.

Dedication

This book is lovingly dedicated to my fellow laborers at Christian Womanhood who have followed me as their new leader, even while they were grieving the loss of Marlene Evans, their former leader.

Thank you for making me feel loved and accepted and for all of your hard work. Thank you also for carrying on the work of Marlene Evans, our mentor and our friend. You are the greatest team in the world, and I love you. During these days of adjustment and grief, thank you for helping me to live on the bright side.

Christian Womanhood Staff

(Left to right)
Back Row:
Jane Grafton
Linda Stubblefield
Dan Wolfe
Front Row:
Nanci Wonson
Rachel Holt
Gina Eyer

Christian Womanhood Spectacular Committee

Back row left to right:
June Ryland
Kris Grafton
Jane Grafton
Belinda Gaona
Nanci Wonson
Middle: Loretta Walker
Cindy Schaap
Dan Wolfe
Front: Gina Eyer
Janice Wolfe

Cathy Kimmel   Linda Stubblefield   Janice Wolfe

    I would like to add a special dedication to Cathy Kimmel, Linda Stubblefield, and Janice Wolfe. While I have been busy adjusting to several changes in my life and writing a book for someone else, they have worked diligently and unselfishly to put together some of my writings for this book. Your kindness has been a precious gift to me. Thank you and I love you!

Acknowledgments

Several people helped in making this book a reality. For quite some time, it has been a dream of Linda Stubblefield's to see my *Christian Womanhood* articles compiled into a book. Her dream became a reality! Thank you, Dan and Janice Wolfe, for reading the manuscript carefully and making editorial suggestions.

Thank you, Cathy Kimmel, for entering all of the corrections carefully.

The book then went back to Linda Stubblefield who designed the content and the cover. She then gave the book to me; and after reading 90 pages, I became very excited about the material and came up with the title, *Living on the Bright Side!*

Our *Christian Womanhood* proofreader, Rena Fish, is a blessing to all of us as she finds time to carefully read our manuscripts. Rena is a wife, mother of three, and teaches at Hyles-Anderson College. Thank you, Rena!

Lastly, thank you, dear ladies of First Baptist Church of Hammond, who have encouraged me greatly through the early days of being the pastor's wife. Your notes and words have been like a healing balm and have helped me to live on the bright side.

Table of Contents

THE FOUR S'S OF THE RESURRECTED LIFE 11-32
*It's Not About Dying ~ It's Really Just a Submission Thing ~
A Tribute to Selflessness ~ We've Got Spirit, Yes, We Do... ~
"S" Is for Satisfaction ~ Only Jesus Can Satisfy*

"FEAR NOT..." 33-56
*Fret Not, Neither Be Dismayed ~ "Fear Not, for I Am
with Thee" ~ Don't Try to Figure It Out! ~ No Regrets! ~
It's a Trap! ~ Let Not Your Heart Be Troubled*

BUILDING AND GROWING RELATIONSHIPS 57-78
*Principles for Relationships ~ The Simple Life ~
What I Have Learned About Friendship ~
Please Read My Billboard ~ You Must Be God's Kid!*

LIVING ON THE BRIGHT SIDE AS A PREACHER'S WIFE . . .79-112
*Making the Valley a Well ~ Feeling Insignificant
or Unworthy ~ When You Feel Afraid ~
Overcoming Self-Pity ~ Triumphing Over Loneliness
and Insecurity ~ Practical Solutions for the Problem
of Loneliness ~ Tips for the Lonely Preacher's Wife ~
Conquering Giants—A Lesson for the Pastor's Wife*

LIVING ON THE BRIGHT SIDE AS A PREACHER'S KID . . .113-136
Danger! Rough Road Ahead! ~

Living on the Bright Side!

~ 10 ~

LIVING ON THE BRIGHT SIDE AS A PREACHER'S KID ...113-136
*The Importance of Meekness ~ Teaching Meekness
to Preachers' Kids ~ Longsuffering and Forebearance/
Unity and Peace ~ What I Have Learned About Crosses*

BALANCE: REARING CHILDREN ~ SERVING GOD 137-160
*The Busyness of Life ~ Loving People When You Are Busy ~
When a Schedule Is Too Busy ~ Thoughts on Recession ~
The Best Thing You Can Do for Your Child*

LIVING ON THE BRIGHT SIDE AS A GODLY WIFE 161-178
*Different, but Not Inferior ~ How to Protect Your Mind ~
What It Means to Be Grave ~ Faithfulness*

LEARNING COMPASSION 179-214
*The Ministry of Encouragement ~ Crybabies ~
When Christians Are Hurting ~ When Christians
Are Straying ~ Put It in the Headlines! ~
How Not to Quit Soul Winning*

DEALING WITH TEMPTATION 215-230
*Temptations Women Face ~ Meeting Your Needs Your Way ~
Proving Ourselves ~ The Desire for Position*

WALKING WITH GOD ON THE BRIGHT SIDE 231-253
*Build Up Yourself ~ Learning to Love ~
What I Am Learning About Love ~ Like a Sister ~
When God Is Enough*

The Four S's
of
a Resurrected Life

Submission

Selflessness

Spirit

Satisfaction

It's Not About Dying

Several years ago I was having a hard time "dying to self" about a particular matter in my life. Then, during my daily devotions, I came across this verse in Romans. *"For if we have been planted together in the likeness of his death, we shall be also in the likeness of his resurrection."* (Romans 6:5)

I began to wonder why I had not been focusing more on the other side of dying to self—that is, the resurrected life. Suddenly, dying to self in my particular situation made more sense and became easier. I thought of this illustration:

For many years, my children and I planted a vegetable garden together. After several years, I retired from vegetable gardening and began to work only with flowers. My busy schedule needed a break.

Jaclynn, however, refused to give up vegetable gardening, and this became her "baby" for the next few summers. One summer, Jaclynn decided to add something new to her garden; she planted sunflowers. Because of lack of space, Jaclynn only planted two sunflower plants. And in just a matter of days, a rabbit, raccoon, or something ate one of the plants. All summer long, Jaclynn nurtured just one sunflower plant.

When Jaclynn finished planting her garden, she did not run into the house crying about the poor little seeds that had to "die to self." She instead ran in and exclaimed, "Mom, I finished planting my garden, and I planted two sunflower plants."

We were both enthusiastic about our sunflowers. When we lost the first plant, I hoped that the growth of the only remaining plant would be worth our enthusiasm.

The truth is, the planting of the sunflower was a very sad time for the sunflower. Its roots were buried beneath the soil. (It's hard to break up the ground down there, you know.) The sunflower roots had to bear the earth's elements, uncomfortable as they can sometimes be, and the seeds had to rot and die. But Jaclynn and I were not concerned—even in the least. We anticipated the growth and the beauty that this death would bring forth. And bring forth beauty it did...

Yes, we only had one sunflower in our garden, but that sunflower grew to be over six feet tall, and at one time, it contained 32 blooms! I had my picture taken with the sunflower; Jaclynn had her picture taken with the sunflower; Brother Schaap even had his picture taken with the sunflower. (This took a little more coaxing!) All three of us had our picture taken with the sunflower, and Kenny...refused the opportunity. All during the fall, our pictures with the sunflower hung on my refrigerator door.

And so it is with dying to self. When you are a preacher's wife, you must die to a lot of things. You cannot seek wealth first and all of the material things that others enjoy. You cannot claim your husband and your children for your own satisfaction as you encourage them to serve the Lord. You cannot always get your own way. You have to die to your own desires time and time again—the ministry comes first, you know. Do we then have a right to say, "Poor me!"? Not on your life!!

Instead we say, "LUCKY, LUCKY ME. I GET TO LIVE THE RESURRECTED LIFE!" I should say "blessed," but sometimes "lucky" just seems like the perfect word to describe how I feel. Every time I have experienced a death to self, God has made something beautiful come from it.

So Christian wives and mothers, and preachers' wives in particular, the next time you are struggling with dying to self, don't just think about an old rugged cross. Look just beyond it to an empty tomb. Don't think about a rotted seed buried beneath the ground; instead, think of a six-foot-tall sunflower with 32 blooms!

Then go ahead and die to self. No, instead, decide to go ahead and live the resurrected life. LUCKY, LUCKY YOU! I don't know what God is going to make of you in your resurrected life, but I know that you are going to be beautiful!

It's Really Just a Submission Thing!

I was talking to a lady in her early thirties who had just lost her husband of eight years. He died of a rare disease when he was just 35 years old, leaving her with four children, ages five and under.

This lady was sharing with me the truths she was learning from a very old book that was written to widows. The author taught that the secret to handling grief was to submit to God's will for your life. He also taught that it takes humility to submit to God's will. I was thankful that these truths were shared with me...and also a little bit convicted about my own lack of submission to circumstances much less difficult than the death of a husband.

As this lady spoke, my mind wandered back to a valley in my own life. I went through a phase in my life where the "Devil seemed to be riding on my shoulder." I remember crying and pleading with God to give me power over the Devil and feeling powerless to deal with the spiritual oppression I was experiencing. I was disappointed in myself and in God, which is always foolish, of course.

A few weeks later, I sat in a chapel service and heard Dr. Dennis Corle preach. He referred to the verse found in James 4:7b, "...*Resist the devil, and he will flee from you.*" He went on to say something like this: "Before you can have power over the Devil, you must first do what the first part of James 4:7 says, "*Submit yourselves therefore to God...*"

I then understood my dilemma. God pointed out to me that there was something in my life about which I was rebelling. I was not submitting to God's will for my life in a particular area. I went to my husband's office, and alone I fell on my knees. I told God that I was submitting myself to everything in my life that was a part of His will for me, whether or not I liked it.

That was the beginning of a journey which led me out of one of the most baffling struggles of my adult years. The Devil "climbed off of my shoulder." I feel powerful through Christ against Satan's attacks on my soul and spirit.

Before we can have power against the Devil as promised in James 4:7b, we must submit as is commanded in James 4:7a. Let me go a step further: Before we can submit to God's will for our lives, we must heed the commandment of James 4:6b which says, *"Wherefore he saith, God resisteth the proud, but giveth grace unto the humble."* Our pride causes us to resist God's will for our lives when He is asking us to accept something that hurts us.

Perhaps you feel like I sometimes do—ashamed that you have such difficulty accepting your negative circumstances when people like the widow mentioned earlier in this chapter so gracefully accepted the death of a husband. Yet God is not asking you or me to accept this widow's lot in life. He is asking us to accept what is His will for us. I spend a lot of time with teenagers these days, so please allow me to put it in teenage "lingo." *It's really just a submission thing!*

I now have a new custom in my prayer life. Each morning I pray something like this before I begin my day: *Dear Lord, I submit myself to all of the things in my life, my husband's life, and my children's lives that are Your will that I don't particularly like.*

As my children become adults, I don't want to be a controlling, possessive mother. Because of this, I send them to their dad to make decisions. Sometimes those decisions are not like the ones I would have made. But I submit myself to them and to the will of my husband. Why? Because without submission, I have no power against the Devil's attacks upon my soul and my spirit.

As I stated in the first chapter, I could say to myself, "Poor, poor me! I have to die to self and become submissive." Yet, I keep discovering that God and my husband are awfully smart as they direct my life and the lives of our children.

Instead, I find myself saying, "Lucky, lucky me! I get to live the resurrected life." I do not see a cross; I see an empty tomb. And I do not see a dirty, rotten seed buried in the ground; instead, I see a six-foot-tall sunflower with 32 blooms!

Remember ladies, before you can live the resurrected life, you must first *"submit yourselves therefore to God."* It's really just a submission thing!

A Tribute to Selflessness

One fall semester at Hyles-Anderson College, my daughter was privileged to take the "Christian Womanhood" class taught by the late Mrs. Marlene Evans. "Mom," Jaclynn said, "Mrs. Evans told us in class that she is planning many special things for her daughter Joy and her family as they come home from the mission field. Mrs. Evans is concerned that Brother Jeff Ryder, Joy, and the children have a good time, even if perhaps Mrs. Evans has to be on chemotherapy at that time."

It was exciting to see Jeff and Joy Ryder and their beautiful children when they arrived home from Papua New Guinea that December for a year-long furlough.

"Jaclynn," I asked, "Do you see anything unusual about this picture? Most women (like myself, I'm afraid), if afflicted with cancer, would be worrying about whether or not they would be able to enjoy their children when they came home from furlough. They might even feel sorry for themselves. Mrs. Evans seems to be putting the focus completely on whether or not others will be enjoying themselves."

It is no wonder that I had heard Dr. Wendell Evans describe his wife, Marlene Evans, as being the most unselfish person he knew.

Selflessness is another key "S" word to living a resurrected life. This is why I pray the following prayer each morning to the Lord as I present myself to Him: "Dear Lord, Help me to take myself out of all things all day long today."

Often as we make decisions in life, we find ourselves confused about what is right or wrong to do. In my own life, when faced with such a confusion, I find that taking myself out of the decision solves my confusion dilemma. As soon as I take myself out of a given decision, the answer becomes clear; and the decision becomes easy to make.

God did not intend our thinking to be full of confusion. Living the Christian life is not difficult. It is not difficult to understand what principles are right to live by according to the Bible. But living the Christian life is hard because it requires selflessness, and selflessness is the constant challenge of the flesh. Allow me to illustrate:

Some time ago my husband asked me to do him a favor while he was at home. I was very tired and looked at him as if to say, "Do it yourself."

One of the children looked at Brother Schaap and said, "I'll do it." I was convicted! I immediately recognized in myself a selfish attitude. I decided to do something about it.

Since that evening, I have strived every day to do one thing for my husband that is out of the routine. It may be giving him a card or a love note. It may be giving him a back massage, a hand massage, or a foot massage. (Don't knock it until you have tried it!) It may be stopping by his office with a favorite treat, drink, or magazine.

Some days I may do several things, but very few days have passed when I have not done at least one thing out of the ordinary for my husband. Cleaning his house, washing and ironing his clothes, and cooking his meals do not count. It has to be something out of the ordinary. I enjoyed the results so much that I began the same process with my children.

Does my husband need a card from me? No, he already has hundreds in his collection from our marriage which began in 1979. Does he need me to "bother" him during a busy day at the office to bring him a favorite drink? No, probably not. Does he need a back rub? He could live without it. (He would argue with that statement.)

It is I who need to do these things. I have found that this aggressive method for fighting selfishness has given me a servant's heart (another "S" word, I might add). In fact not long after I tried my new plan, my husband asked me to get something for him. He stopped himself in mid-sentence and said, "No, that's okay; I'll get it myself."

When I heard him say, "That's okay; I'll get it myself," I literally ran through the house to get it before he did. We both had a good chuckle, and he left for work. I returned to my work and thought to myself, "Now, that's better; I like that much better than my attitude of a few weeks ago." Aggressive service is changing my selfish attitude into an attitude of selflessness.

God often uses His grace to create a three-dimensional picture of His attributes through human lives and through human suffering. Mrs. Evans was just such a picture. Her life was a living color picture of Jesus' sacrificial attribute of selflessness.

One of the disadvantages (and advantages) of having wonderful parents is that I rarely go to people outside of my family for counsel. I have asked myself through the years, however, "If I did not have my parents, where would I turn?" I believe my husband and I could turn to Dr. and Mrs. Evans. I not only love them, but I trust them.

Never have I seen a woman's Christianity validated through her suffering as much as I saw it in the life of Marlene Evans. Her life also validated the level of her selflessness.

Yet, in order to live the resurrected life, we must take our self out of all things. Yet let us not feel sorry for ourselves. Let us not complain about having to die to self like a rotten seed; instead, let us rejoice that we can live a resurrected life like a six-foot-tall sunflower with 32 blooms.

We've Got Spirit, Yes, We Do; We've Got Spirit, How 'Bout You?

I am not a person who has a naturally beautiful smile. I am actually a rather shy, analytical person and can seem to be frowning when I am actually deep in thought.

When I was in college, a certain young man loved to pass me in the hallway and say, "Cindy, smile! God loves you!" I found this admonition from my fellow student whom I did not know very well to be irritating. I knew in my heart that I loved the Lord and had a walk with Him. "Why do some people have to focus so much on smiles and enthusiasm?" I would ask myself.

Over a decade ago, I heard a sermon preached by Dr. Bob Gray at a Youth Conference in Piedmont, Missouri. Dr. and Mrs. Gray have always been a hero and heroine to me, and it was Dr. Gray whom God used to convict me about my spirit. Through his sermon, I began to understand how important my smile and my enthusiasm are.

Sure, I may love the Lord, my church, my husband, and so forth deep down in my heart. My love may even go deeper than the love of a more boisterous Christian. But it remains true that no one will know I love the Lord, my church, my husband, or anyone else, unless I show it with my spirit.

When I watch our son Kenny play basketball, I watch him with my spirit. No, I have never yelled at the referee or at the other team. But when Kenny does something right on the basketball court, no one must wonder whether I am for him or against him. I love Kenny very deep down in my heart, but when he scores a basket, my love comes bubbling up to the surface and out of my very enthusiastic mouth.

Many times I have left a basketball game saying that I am going to be more quiet next time. Never yet have I left a basketball game having kept that promise!

You see, when we really love someone, it will be evidenced by our spirit. It must be evidenced by our spirit, or God is the only One Who will see our love. Our light will not shine before men.

One of the preachers who travels with our Hyles-Anderson College summer tour groups told a group in a meeting I attended something like this: "I have never been in a church that was growing and winning souls where there was not a pastor's wife who was friendly and had a great spirit. Wherever I have found an unfriendly pastor's wife, I have found a small, dead church."

Now I am not trying to blame the pastor's wife for the seeming success or failure of her husband's church. But I must say that the abovementioned admonition had an effect on me. I would never want my spirit to prevent God from using my husband in whatever way God has planned for him. And I know that the Devil fights the spirit of a preacher's wife; I know that he fights my spirit. Allow me to share with you some areas I have worked on since hearing Dr. Gray's sermon.

1. **Smile!** I actually practiced smiling when I was alone in my house, doing such things as vacuuming. I still struggle with looking too serious, especially when I am intrigued by a point in the preacher's sermon. But I am constantly working on my smile. If someone's joining your church were dependent upon your smile, would they even consider it?

2. **Be friendly!** I have learned from my husband to have a tremendous love for all people. One of the greatest things I learned from my father is not to be a respecter of persons.

Though I am shy by nature, I strive to give a warm smile and a friendly greeting to everyone I pass at church or anywhere else.

I strive to be as friendly as possible to the special needs people whom I pass at church or to the bus kid, even the obnoxious one, as I would be to one of the church leaders. If I feel that someone is unfriendly to me, I ask the Lord to help me to find ways to be extra friendly to that person.

3. Sing! When I am in church, I strive to do what my pastor admonishes us to do and that is to really think about the words when I sing the congregational songs. It is humorous and yet sad to look around and watch the countenances of people as they sing such songs as "I Am So Happy in the Service of the King." They should be singing, "I Am So Grumpy in the Service of the King."

4. Respond. One of the key words to being a good wife is the word "respond." This is also a key word in reflecting your love for the Lord, your pastor, your church, and others. Respond to the joke that is told, to the story the pastor gives, to the invitation, and to the entire church service with a response that shows your support.

I suppose one of the reasons why I *chose* to be introverted and quiet in college is because I did not like show-offs. But when my parents faced some battles in their ministry, I realized that "showing off" is not always a bad thing.

At first, I wanted to run away from my parents' battles. Then I heard that life-changing sermon from Dr. Bob Gray, and I decided it was my turn to "show off!" It was my turn to show my support for my parents. If I did not show my support for my parents through my enthusiastic spirit, how would anyone know that I stood for them?

That is when I began writing articles and books. I was hoping to "show off" so that my parents' ministry could be reflected in a more positive way. That was when I began to practice smiling (though I had never felt more like crying). I picked up my cross of responsibility and began to take on the challenge of supporting my pastor, parents, and church through a more friendly, enthusiastic spirit.

This is something with which my shy, serious nature still struggles and on which I must work daily. The more the Lord uses my husband, the more pressure I feel on my spirit. Yet, I do not see this as a cross; rather, I feel that I am privileged to reflect the resurrected life. And I do not want my spirit to be like a dirty, rotten seed that is buried far beneath the ground. Instead, I want it to bloom like a six-foot-tall sunflower with 32 blooms.

Go ahead and try it! Reflect your love with an enthusiastic spirit. Don't cause those who pass by you today to have to wonder whether or not you even like them. And I pass on to you the wonderful advice of a young college boy I once knew: "SMILE! GOD LOVES YOU!"

"S" Is
for Satisfaction

Our dining room table is surrounded by three large windows. A couple of times a bird has tried to fly into those windows when they were closed. One bird knocked his head against the glass over and over for several weeks. Finally, he seemed to give up and realized he was trying to go somewhere that was not his place!

Several years ago I heard Mrs. Carla Likens speak. She is the wife of the Youth Director at Shawnee Baptist Church of Louisville, Kentucky, Dr. Reno Likens. Carla gave an excellent lesson to the girls of the Shawnee Youth Conference from Proverbs 27:8, *"As a bird that wandereth from her nest, so is a man that wandereth from his place."* This verse reminded me of the fourth "S" of the resurrected life—satisfaction. Every preacher's wife must have satisfaction as one of her virtues.

First of all, a preacher's wife must be satisfied with her place, both spiritually and physically. A preacher's wife's place cannot be a competitive place. She cannot decide to choose her place based upon what she sees someone else doing. Her choice of a place should not be based on her desire to prove that she can succeed where someone else has failed. Rather, her place should be chosen based upon the purpose that God has for her.

I am 100 percent convinced that my main purpose in life is to be a helper to my husband, Dr. Jack Schaap. Second only to that has been my purpose of rearing my two children from infancy into mature Christians. Because this is my purpose, my place has been to stay mainly at home.

My place is not working as a doctor, as a lawyer, in a secular career, or even in a full-time ministry. I cannot say that I have never left my place since I was married on June 1, 1979. I have thought about working full time and about adding more than I should to my life. I have tried things that have not turned out to be an aid, but rather a hindrance to my purpose. When I have tried them, I have felt like that bird trying to fly into my dining room window. I have felt like I was flapping my wings faster and faster, but not flying in any particular direction.

It was then when I returned to my place. I returned to my home where I stayed more frequently so that my busy family could fly to the different places that God had for them. As long as I am in my place, the birds in my nest seem to fly quite fast, high, and smoothly, as I do. But when I leave my place, all of the birds in my nest seem more prone to flap and flap and lose their sense of direction.

I do not resent my place, though it may seem less glamorous even than the places of those with whom I live. Instead, I am satisfied with my place. When I am satisfied with my place, it is exalted. When I resent my place, I "put down" my place before others.

I do not compete in my place, because I not only want to finish the flight. I also want to be sure that I have taken the right flight which God has designed specifically for me. I do not want to run another's race. As Carla Likens so aptly reminded me in her lesson, if I am not in my place, my place will either be left empty or another person will fill it.

I also do not judge the place of others. Someone who is unmarried, has no children, or who is of a different age may have a place that is perfectly fine for them to fill. But that same place could be "out of place" for me. Someone with a less busy family may fill a place that I should not fill. And yes, someone may be out of place, but that is not mine to judge. I simply need to find my place and be satisfied.

Satisfaction is the last "S" which aids in living the resurrected life. It is the tool which helps us to forget about dying to things we cannot have. Satisfaction helps us to enjoy what we do have so that we feel like the richest folks on earth.

As long as I am satisfied with my place, it does not seem like a cold, dark, lonely place underneath the ground. Instead, my place seems like a place where six-foot-tall sunflowers bloom in my heart all year long.

Let's hear it for dying to self. Oops! I mean let's hear it for the resurrected life! God is the only One Who has blessings that can truly satisfy.

Only Jesus Can Satisfy

In 1983, God gave to my husband and me a beautiful house. It is a small house, and it is not a new house—our house was 12 years old when we bought it. But when God gave it to us, I decided that I would be satisfied with the place God had for me until God kicked me out of it. I am sure there is not a week that goes by that I do not say something like this to my family, "I love our house," or "Look at this house. Doesn't it look like a happy family lives here?" I say this because I really want to enjoy what God gives me, and I do not want my husband to feel pressured to buy me a bigger or better house.

When our son was four years old, he said to me, "Mom, I want to live in the house across the street."

"Why?" I asked.

"Because," he answered, "our house is the smallest house in the neighborhood, and that house is the biggest."

"Kenny, do you think that our family has been happy in this house?" I asked.

"Yes."

"Do you know that we would be happy in the house across the street?"

"No."

"Then don't you think it would be silly to move to the house across the street?"

I was trying to teach Kenny that relationships are more important than things.

Our house is surrounded by new subdivisions with enormous new houses. Yet, I have never seen a place where I would rather live than our place.

Oftentimes, God does move a family into a new and large house; I am always happy for them. But I also hope that each one of us will be truly satisfied with the place God has given us and will not always be longing for another one.

A preacher's wife must also be satisfied with her material possessions. I never see a car and wish I could have that one. I am immensely satisfied with the car that I am driving now. I have sometimes turned down generous gifts from people who have sought to be a blessing to me. Why? Because other than helping my husband and children, my *purpose* is to work part time teaching preachers' wives and future preachers' wives. Therefore, my *place* is not to live too extravagantly at such a young age.

My *purpose* is to rear children to serve the Lord. I will handicap them if I create in them an appetite for things that they will not be able to afford in the ministry.

Most importantly of all, I am also handicapping my husband if I cause him to feel that he is not providing enough for me. I have told my husband repeatedly that I do not want him to make me rich; I simply want him to meet my needs. And by the way, he seems to spoil me anyway.

I am not writing about materialism. If we live in America, we are more materialistic than we could even realize. I am writing about *satisfaction.* I am writing about enjoying to the fullest the things that God gives us and not always longing for more. I am writing about running our financial decisions through the sifter of Matthew 6:24, "...*Ye cannot serve God and mammon.*"

I have been spoiled immeasurably by the Lord and those who love me. Yet hopefully, I am not a spoiled "brat." If I have escaped this fate and continue to escape it, the reason will be my satisfaction. My *purpose* helps me to understand to stay in my *place.* My *place* brings me great satisfaction so that I need not judge others nor resent them though their place of ministry or wealth may seem larger than mine.

As I have already mentioned, *satisfaction* is the last "S" which aids in living the resurrected life. It is the tool which helps us to forget about dying to things we cannot have. Satisfaction helps us to enjoy what we do have so that we feel like the richest folks on earth!

"Fear Not..."

Fret Not, Neither Be Dismayed

"*This book of the law shall not depart out of thy mouth; but thou shalt meditate therein day and night, that thou mayest observe to do according to all that is written therein: for then thou shalt make thy way prosperous, and then thou shalt have good success. Have not I commanded thee? Be strong and of a good courage; be not afraid, neither be thou dismayed.*" (Joshua 1:8, 9a)

On April 16, 1998, I began underlining and writing notes every time I would see the words, "fear," "trust," or "faith" in my daily Bible reading. I continued this study for a year, until April 16, 1999. Because I enjoyed this study so much, I began a new study the following April on a different Bible subject.

I began my study on fear because of my husband's advice, and once again he had led me on a very helpful path. I chose the subject of fear because it seemed to be a root sin which is attached to so many other sins, and it seemed attached to so many areas in which I struggle in my spiritual life.

For example, in the Bible the phrase, "*Fear not,*" is often followed by such phrases as, "*be not dismayed,*" or "*be not confounded.*" As I studied the subject of fear, I learned that one of the meanings of the Bible word *dismayed* is depression. Thus God teaches that the root sin of fear leads to depression.

The Bible word *confounded* means confusion. God teaches us that the root sin of fear leads to confusion or poor decision making. I believe that there are basically two root sins which lead to the sin of jealousy. They are pride and fear.

A pastor's wife may feel jealous toward her husband's work with women because she is proud. Her pride may cause her not to want her husband to work with someone who may be more attractive, more intelligent, and so forth. This type of jealousy cannot be cured until the root sin of pride is confessed and given to God properly. (Pride is often a result of lack of proper confidence in one's self.)

On the other hand, a wife may feel jealous because of fear. Perhaps experiences in her past may cause her to fear losing someone she loves to another woman. The jealousy cannot be dealt with until the fear is recognized as sin, confessed, and given to the Lord.

The Bible answers for fear are trust, faith, strength, and courage. Joshua 1:8 and 9 teach us that proper use of the Word of God gives us the strength and courage to fight fear and depression.

I read an article which stated that by the year 2010, the most common physical illness in the United States, second only to heart disease, will be depression. This article also stated that laws are constantly being passed which make it easier and eas-ier for medical doctors to prescribe drugs to people who are depressed.

I realize that there is a time and a place to prescribe some drugs for people who suffer from depression which is a result of injury to the brain. I also realize that I am not to be the judge of such people, and I do not judge these individuals. However, I believe more and more that Christians who have not suffered physical injuries are becoming depressed and turning to drugs such as Prozac before they have properly tried the Word of God.

One of my desires through these chapters on fear is to encourage fundamental Christian ladies to seek the Word of

God and to use it properly in their lives before seeking medical help, psychological help, or even Christian counseling.

So, for the next several chapters I write, I am intending to share with you what I have learned from the great Counselor, the Prince of Peace. Once again He has proven to me that His Living Word is valid and relevant to the problems I face today. How eternally usable are the answers from the Bible.

"Fear Not, for I Am with Thee"

"*Have not I commanded thee? Be strong and of a good courage; be not afraid, neither be thou dismayed: for the LORD thy God is with thee whithersoever thou goest.*" (Joshua 1:9)

As I have studied the Bible on the subject of fear, I have found God's most often used reason for not being afraid is this: "I am with thee." It is as if God is wanting to hear said what every loved one longs to hear from her beloved, "Just to know that You are near me is enough."

I am selfish in my reasons for Bible reading and prayer. I selfishly want the knowledge, as I walk this earth and dwell among mankind, that God is with me in a special way. I ask God to be with me in a special way each morning as I read, memorize, and study my Bible. In my daily prayer time, I beg God to go with me all day long, in everything I do and everywhere I go. The older I become, the more I cherish the thought that God is with me. Just to have Him near me seems more and more to be indeed enough. But this has not always been the case.

Though I have always possessed somewhat of a loner-type nature, there have been times in my life when I feared being alone. When my preacher husband first started traveling, I often took my children to my parents' house and spent the night there. When I was first married, I even feared being alone during the early evening hours (or should I say after dark?!) I planned things to prevent being alone at home after the sun went down.

I already possessed a walk with God, but my faith in God was very immature. I tried to love God and to obey Him, but I lacked the ability to trust Him as I should. He was with me, even back then, as real as He is now. He, of course, was no less powerful in my early adult years than He is now in my middle-aged years. Still, I did not avail myself of the full peace and glory of His presence. I instead wanted to place my trust, as my dad would have said, in someone "who had skin on him."

God, I believe, lovingly chastened me for my sin of fear by leading me through some deeper waters in my life. I waded through a stream created just for me, and no one could pass through it with me. A loving husband and parents stood on the banks of its shores yelling to me that I could make it and throwing me the anchor of the Word of God. Yet, as I passed through deep waters, no one could go through them with me. There was no one with skin on him who could understand my personal trials—not even myself. BUT GOD WAS WITH ME!

I am definitely not whining. My deep waters have been shallow compared to the trials of so many others. And looking back, I realize that I have been blessed. It is wonderful to arrive at a place where it is just you and God.

I have heard my husband preach a sermon where he challenges his audience to notice how many times the verb "see" or some form of it is found in the faith chapter, Hebrews 11. My husband taught me that faith is seeing what others do not see. The people mentioned in Hebrews 11 were unique individuals with their own unique personality weaknesses and sins. Yet they all *"endured, as seeing him who is invisible."* (Hebrews 11:27b)

Those who do not endure or succeed in the Christian life are not necessarily more sinful or weak than those who do.

They simply lack the faith to see what blessings and usefulness God has in store for them.

Those who struggle with fear in their lives need to meditate in this thought: GOD IS WITH ME! When I fear for my husband or for my children or for some other loved one and I realize there is nothing I can do, I picture in my mind God sitting beside my children in school, or I picture God sitting beside my husband in his office. I picture the very hand of God working in their lives, answering my daily prayers, and doing what I cannot do. I do not fear for their futures. Why? GOD IS WITH THEM!

I now stay alone at night when my husband is out of town. If I awaken in the darkness and miss his presence, I look and see that God is filling the bedroom with the glory of His presence. I picture God standing guard at both the front door and the back door (at the same time), and I drift back into peaceful sleep. Why am I not afraid? I know that God is with me! I never allow a day to go by without seeking God's presence. For knowing He is with me is too important to me.

So when you see me in the auditorium of First Baptist Church or in the hallways of Hyles-Anderson College, you may or may not see me with my husband or children. I may or may not be sharing laughter with a friend. But I definitely will not be alone! If you look closely, you will see Someone very well-known and important holding my hand. GOD IS WITH ME!

Don't forget to look beside you, too! God will be standing there! Hold your head high and walk with dignity. You run with the important people.

This is a simple truth—one I was taught since childhood—one I taught my own children. I told my daughter Jaclynn that God ate dinner with us and that He sat in the empty chair at the table. One evening when a guest sat in that chair, four-year-old Jaclynn informed him that he was sitting on God!

This simple childlike truth is used by God more than any other in His Word to teach us how to overcome fear. Yet adults don't seem able to comprehend it. God is with me where I am, and God is with you where you are, even though we may be thousands of miles apart. That sounds more unbelievable than a science-fiction movie. Yet, it takes a lifetime to understand that we are not dealing with science fiction. The presence of God is reality!

God is with me! God is with you!
Never, never, never be afraid!

Don't Try to Figure It Out!

"*Trust in the LORD with all thine heart; and lean not unto thine own understanding.*" (Proverbs 3:5)

I have a very analytical mind. I don't want to just know that something is wrong; I want to know *why* it is wrong. One of my very favorite things to analyze is people. I don't want to just know what they do; I want to know *why* they do what they do. I don't just want to see their actions and hear their words; I want to analyze *what* they are thinking.

Analytical minds may belong to great philosophers, great writers, even great scientists. But a mind that is analytical in the wrong things can become possessed with fear. The wrong kind of analytical mind can turn a great preacher's wife into a useless one.

It is wise for all of us to learn how to avoid analyzing the wrong things, for all of us are sometimes too analytical. The following statements are examples that may reveal that a person is analyzing the wrong things:

- "I don't think anyone likes me." (Just why do you think that?)

- "Do you think she was telling me the truth?" (Now that you have asked her, and maybe you shouldn't have, why don't you believe her?)

- "I wonder what she meant by that." (How could you possibly know without asking her?)

- "I wonder what people think about the mistake I made when I sang that song." (If you knew they were thinking critically, could you undo the mistake?)

- "I could never speak in public. I might say the wrong thing, and people might criticize me." (But what about the possibility that you could say the right thing and God might use you to help someone?)

- "I could never write a book or an article to help someone. Others might not think I am qualified. Besides, if I wrote something I shouldn't, it would forever be in print!" (But what if God wants to use you as a writer?)

- "I could never be friendly with her. She might think I have ulterior motives." (But what if she needs your friendship?)

- "I could never be a good preacher's wife. People might see my weaknesses and reject me." (But what if your husband needs you?)

I trust these statements illustrate to you how paralyzing the wrong kind of analytical mind can be. It is wrong to *"lean unto thine own understanding,"* especially when it comes to analyzing people, their thoughts, and their motives. The result of such analyzing is fear. One becomes afraid to do anything for God.

The cure for the wrong kind of analytical mind is to *"Trust in the LORD with all thine heart."* You may ask, "Mrs. Schaap, do you ever worry or fear what people might think?" Of course I do! In fact, most of the aforementioned analytical statements have at one time or another been formulated in my own analytical mind.

How Have I Avoided Them?

1. **I have recognized that these and others like them are unfair statements.** They are unfair to myself, and they are unfair to others.

2. **When I have recognized them for what they are, I have proceeded to practice trusting in the Lord.** I have prayed and asked the Lord to defend me to others, and then I have trusted the Lord to use me to be a blessing to others in spite of my many mistakes.

3. **Lastly, I have decided to give myself and others the benefit of the doubt.** I believe people love me and see good in me, and I believe God can use me to love them in return, even when people see that I am human.

As a preacher's wife, allow me to exhort you future preachers' wives to go ahead and jump into the ministry with both feet, trusting in the Lord with all your heart and leaning not to your own understanding.

P .S.   I hope you know what I meant by that!

No Regrets!

When I graduated from high school, I remember telling my father that I had no regrets. Yes, I did make some mistakes in high school. And if there was a time when I could have had regrets, it was during my freshman and sophomore years of high school. But during the beginning of my junior year, God changed my life. I finished high school feeling I had been spared some tragedy and had made some very important right choices at a critical time in my life…and I had no regrets.

Before walking down the aisle on my wedding day, I remember again telling my dad that I had no regrets. I had hurt my parents from time to time. Yet I left their home feeling I had tried to right wrongs, and to the best of my ability, I had tried to be close to them and to honor them…and I had no regrets.

On June 1, 2003, my husband and I celebrated our twenty-fourth wedding anniversary. I cannot count the number of times I have thought about or looked at the man I married on June 1, 1979, and said to myself "no regrets." I know that I married the man God made for me to marry. Have I been a perfect wife? No, I have made many mistakes. Is my husband perfect? Well, almost. We are imperfect, but during each bend in the road, the Lord has led us in the right direction. We have been committed to walk the path together…and I have no regrets.

On May 21, 1999, our oldest child graduated from high school. In September, she packed her belongings and moved all the way to Crown Point, Indiana, (15 minutes away) and became a Hyles-Anderson College dormitory student at the advice of her pastor. I saw her often, maybe once a week.

Because I was a very involved mother, her move to the dormitory was still an adjustment for me.

When my daughter Jaclynn was born in 1981, I was only 21 years old. I had heard many young mothers complain about how much work children were and exclaim how much they looked forward to their growing older. I also heard many older ladies as they admonished me to "Enjoy them while you have them—they grow up so fast."

I often wondered why the *younger* ladies couldn't enjoy them while they had them instead of the *older* ladies who did not have them anymore. I decided that I would take the advice of the older ladies and enjoy my children while I had them. Then when they were older, I would exclaim how much work they were and how glad I am they are grown.

When Jaclynn was nine years old, I wrote a book entitled *A Wife's Purpose.* After the book was published, I received invitations to speak at ladies' meetings all across the country. I took a few, but I was very careful how many I accepted. One pastor told me that he liked my philosophy on marriage and child rearing (God's philosophy, I hope!) so much that he wanted me to speak at his church every year. I remember wondering if I would even have a marriage and children if I spoke at his church and others every year.

When Jaclynn became a teenager, she became so busy that I began to miss something important every time I was out of town, even though I did not travel often. I also began to inconvenience my husband and his ministry. I asked my husband if I could put my traveling on hold for a while, and he said he had been praying about how to ask me to do so. We were definitely in one mind about the matter, so I stopped traveling. I did not miss anything, but I hated saying "no" to the preachers' wives whom I had come to love. I have enjoyed being a mother to Jaclynn and Kenny; and as Jaclynn left our home for the first time, I felt that I had not missed a thing...and I had no regrets.

I do not wish to brag! If I have made right choices, it has been the result of a walk with God. From Him is where every-thing good comes! And I have made mistakes—boy, I have made mistakes!! I suppose if rewards were given for mistakes, I could get "The Daughter Mistake Award," "The Wife Mistake Award," and "The Mother Mistake Award" all in one. Yet those words kept passing through my sentimental mind over and over as I shopped for items for the dormitory. *No regrets...no regrets...no regrets!*

Why do I wish to share these feelings with you?

1. Because I enjoy sharing each stage of my life with oth-ers. But that is not the only reason.

2. Because I also wish to admonish and to encourage other ladies to "enjoy them while you can; they grow up so fast." There were times when I was teaching the Bible to my two year old, that I felt like life was passing me by. I sometimes wondered if my ministry at that time was so small because I was just a weak Christian.

Years later, I say with the older ladies (Am I one of them?) to enjoy your children while you can. To us middle-aged moth-ers, the most noble briefcase is a diaper bag; and the most graceful walk is the walk of a mother with a diaper bag on her shoulder, a baby in one arm, and a toddler holding the other hand. Take each step of this part of your life in dignity—they grow up so fast!

3. I wrote these feelings also as a reminder to my own daughter of what she should prepare for in college. For a lady, college should not be about preparing for success. Rather, it should be about preparing to sacrifice. For a lady, college should not be about preparing for one's own ministry as much as it should be about preparing to build someone else's.

I wrote to remind Jaclynn about her heritage. Jaclynn, your Grandma Hyles is one of the greatest examples of sacrifice of all time as she helped your grandfather build the great First Baptist Church, and she was at home for me while I was growing up in spite of her busy role as first lady of our church.

Your Grandma Schaap literally gave a portion of her life and some of her health to help your Grandpa Schaap build his business. She drove the machinery or brought lemonade and kept dinner warm until ten o'clock at night so Grandpa could be successful.

Your Aunt Kristi may be the best example of all. Though in terrible health, she has been her husband's partner in the dry-cleaning business all of these years. She has worked a hot press, ironing clothes on summer days because she is devoted to the dreams of her family.

I could go on and on. Jaclynn, ours is not a heritage of success but a heritage of sacrifice (which led to success in the abovementioned cases, by the way). Success is not our goal, though it may be a by-product. *Being there* is our goal.

Why have I written a chapter on child rearing in the midst of a series on fear? Because I find though I have no regrets, I fear my children's future. Will they turn out right? Now that their choices are more and more their own, will they also be able to say 20 years from now, "no regrets"?

In my Bible study on fear, I have found several promises for our children. I want to remind myself of some now and share them with you.

• "*Ye that fear the* LORD, *trust in the* LORD: *he is their help and their shield. The* LORD *hath been mindful of us: he will bless us; he will bless the house of Israel; he will bless the house of Aaron. He will bless them that fear the* LORD, *both small and great. The* LORD *shall increase you more and more, you and your children.*" (Psalm 115:11–14)

- *"And all thy children shall be taught of the LORD; and great shall be the peace of thy children."* (Isaiah 54:13)

- *"Thou shalt know also that thy seed shall be great..."* (Job 5:25)

There are so many promises God has for us in His Word, but these are some I claim specifically for our children. It is wrong to fear for our children. Instead we should trust in the Lord. It is wonderful to know that the same God Who has led us thus far will be there to lead them to make the right choices in their lives...so that they too can say, "no regrets."

Remember, young mothers, enjoy them while you can; they grow up fast! Remember, old mothers, they are a lot of trouble; aren't you glad they are grown!

It's a Trap!

$\mathcal{O}ur$ family owns a yellow Labrador retriever. The McCullough family raised Labs, and they gave us this beautiful and valuable dog. We named her Dusty Rose of Texas. She is a purebred, and her name is longer than mine. However, we simply call her Dusty.

Dusty is my son Kenny's dog, but the rest of our family loves her as much as Kenny does. When my husband and I walk Dusty on occasion, he often exclaims, "She's beautiful! She's beautiful!" (I remind my husband that he used to talk about me that way!)

On summer evenings, Jaclynn and I walk Dusty two miles through our neighborhood. We walk quickly for exercise, and when we reach the undeveloped property at the end of our street, we take Dusty off of her leash and let her run.

Often I bring out the leftover food that is about to spoil, and I reward Dusty as she performs her tricks. Dusty can sit, lie down, shake hands, fetch, and roll over. I am not sure about my child rearing, but my dog rearing is impressive!

Sometimes, though, Dusty is rebellious when it comes time to return to her pen, especially if she feels she has not been out long enough. Such was the case one night. I solved this problem by bringing out a piece of foil which had formerly been covering a piece of pizza. Though the pizza was gone, the foil *smelled* like it had pizza in it. I held the foil over the pen, and Dusty walked inside. I then shut the pen door, locked it, and walked away with the empty piece of foil. Dusty had been fooled and trapped and left with nothing to show for it. I should have felt guilty, but instead I walked away feeling very intelligent.

I thought of this experience this morning as I was thinking of Proverbs 29:25 which says, *"The fear of man bringeth a snare: but whoso putteth his trust in the LORD shall be safe."* The Bible teaches us that it is wrong to fear man. We are to fear God rather than man. God teaches us that the fear of man is a snare or a trap. It can trap us into situations that are not best for us, and it can leave us empty, with nothing to show for our decisions.

What kind of people need to guard against fearing man? Insecure people need to be extra careful. I believe that 99.9 percent of people are insecure to some degree, so we all need to guard against the fear of man.

How Is the Fear of Man Evidenced?

1. The fear of man is evidenced by excessive need for approval. Though I want to please people, I cannot make my decisions based upon what people will think of me. I attend a church with thousands of people. I cannot please all of them all of the time. Therefore, I must make my decisions, first of all, upon the Word of God. Secondly, I make my decisions according to the advice of my most God-like authority, my husband.

If it is in my power not to offend people by the way I dress and so forth, I do my best not to offend anyone. When the Bible or my husband's/pastor's advice offends someone or is misunderstood, I do not fear man. I do not worry about what people think. It's a trap!

2. The fear of man is evidenced by excessive desire for money or material things. I have a home that is lovely; I believe that is pleasing to God and to my family. I decided a long time ago not to get involved in the "bigger-and-better race" however. If I try to intimidate, impress, or win man's approval by my house, my clothing, or my jewelry, I evidence fear of man. None of these things in themselves is wrong, but I must keep my desire for them in check. I do not wish to impress people by bragging about the size of my bank account. To do so would reveal the fear of man. It's a trap!

4. The fear of man is evidenced by a need for exclusivity. That is the need to be loved by a person so much that you become jealous of that person's friendships with others. I have shared my parents with literally thousands of people, maybe tens of thousands. I tried to avoid seeking to prove to any of those people that my relationship with my parents was more exclusive or loyal than theirs was.

3. The fear of man is evidenced by strife and contention. Proverbs 13:10 says, *"Only by pride cometh contention."* I have made a decision that I will only separate from friends if I disagree with their doctrines or their standards, or if they themselves are causing strife or contention. I use the authority of my husband/pastor to help me with these decisions.

But if someone says, "If you associate with one person, you cannot be a friend with another person," I immediately smell the fear of man. I refuse to separate from a child of God based on the fear of man. It's a trap!

Let Not Your Heart Be Troubled

When I was expecting my first child, I took Lamaze classes. A Christian lady, Mrs. Barbara Wing, came to my home and taught me how to endure labor pains without the use of painkilling drugs. One of the principles this lady taught me was to have a focal point. Mrs. Wing encouraged me to bring a picture on which I could focus to hang on the wall of the hospital birthing room. This picture was to be my focal point—the thing I would concentrate upon to help me *not* to think about the pain. Mrs. Wing suggested I bring a picture that would evoke positive thoughts and a peaceful spirit.

I was reminded of the focal point idea the other day when I was reflecting upon Psalm 112:7 which says, *"He shall not be afraid of evil tidings: his heart is fixed, trusting in the LORD."* God tells us in John 14:1a to *"Let not your heart be troubled."* In other words, we are not supposed to *allow* ourselves to be upset or afraid.

I have always struggled with the sin of worry. I remember my dad often putting my childish worries to rest in his own special way, and then I recall his gently reminding me that worry is a sin. It has taken me years, however, to understand exactly how to "let not my heart be troubled."

I am learning how to avoid the sin of worry by fixing my heart upon a focal point. Faith in God is the focal point to which I fix my heart each morning, and I *refuse* to allow my heart or mind to be distracted from that faith. How do I achieve this? Let me give you some ideas.

1. I read the Bible first thing each morning, underlining verses which help me—especially in the area of fear.

2. I memorize two new verses in the Bible each day. I happen to be memorizing John chapter 14 at this writing, which has some great verses on the subject of fear.

3. I write down lessons I learn each morning in a notebook I am formulating on the subject of fear.

4. Each morning as I pray, I ask the Holy Spirit to renew my mind. I ask Him not to allow me to think negatively all day long. I ask Him to help my thoughts to be calm, peaceful, positive, and full of faith in Jesus (my focal point) all day long.

5. I have a list of Bible promises which I quote to the Lord each morning in prayer time as I ask Him to meet particular needs in my life.

6. I listen to sermon tapes and praise music much of the time when I am alone.

7. I sing out loud much during each day, choosing songs that strengthen my faith in Jesus, my focal point.

8. I ask God to help me to see Him each day in both small and miraculous ways, and then I look around all day, trying to find where He might demonstrate Himself.

9. I ask God to speak to me each day, and I listen carefully in church and other places, knowing that God will have a personal message just from God to Cindy. God and my pastor never let me down in this area.

10. I praise God each time I hear or see something beautiful, believing it came personally from God to me. Praise is a wonderful way to reveal your faith to God and to others, and it is also a wonderful method for strengthening your faith.

11. I avoid sin and worldliness, if for no other reason, because it distracts me from my faith in Jesus, my focal point.

12. I return to my previously underlined verses, and I

return to God again in prayer several times throughout the day. I ask the Holy Spirit to again fill me and to renew my mind once more to thoughts of my faith in Jesus, my focal point.

There are days when it is easy to think positively and to focus on my faith. There are other days when Satan himself seems to bombard my mind with all that is negative and fearful. On those days, I fix my heart and focus the eyes of my soul upon my faith in Jesus with extra intensity, as if I were trying to be hypnotized. I sing louder; I mentally list things for which I should be thankful; I do all of the above-listed items with even more determination. Why? Because it is indeed a sin to worry.

Life is for ministering to people. People cannot make it spiritually unless they have faith in God. We, as ladies, can lead other women to faith. But first of all, we must get alone each day and use whatever amount of "alone time" we have to focus our faith in Jesus. After doing so, our own lives can be a focal point, causing others to fix themselves upon faith in Jesus Christ.

Dear Lord,
When people watch my life, may I be a focal point which helps them to forget their pain. May my life evoke in others a positive spirit and peaceful thoughts. May I remind others of faith in Jesus and of the limitless power of God. Amen.

"Peace I leave with you, my peace I give unto you: not as the world giveth, give I unto you. Let not your heart be troubled, neither let it be afraid." (John 14:27)

Building
and
Growing Relationships

Principles for Relationships

There are four principles which have helped me in all of my relationships. Please allow me to share them with you.

1. Life is relationships. This should be obvious to all of us, but it is something about which we all need to be reminded constantly, especially as Americans. Our success in life really has nothing to do with the clothes we wear or the house in which we live or even the jobs we do. All of these are only important as they affect the people in our lives and our relationships.

2. The Devil fights relationships. Because the success or failure of our lives depends solely upon the quality of our relationships with other people, the Devil fights our relationships. He most fights those relationships which are the most important to us.

For example, when I was a child living at home, my relationship with my parents was my most important relationship. My success in my Christian life depended more on my feelings toward my parents than any other thing. This is why the Devil fights children getting along with their parents and parents getting along with their children.

Now that I am married, my most important relationship is that with my husband. Because of this, the Devil is going to fight my feelings toward him more than he fights my feelings toward anyone else. Though I am happily married and have written and taught on marriage, I readily admit that the Devil fights my marriage relationship. I handle this by recognizing that my husband is not my enemy—the Devil is. When I can recognize that it is the Devil who is my enemy, I can unite with my husband in fighting him, even when we disagree.

Teenage girl, your parents are not your enemies. The Devil knows how important your parents are to you whether you do or not. Therefore, he fights your feelings toward them. Resist him by refusing to act rebelliously toward them.

Parents, that confused and disorganized teenager is not your enemy. The Devil does not want you to be close to her, so he allows her to get on your nerves. Resist the Devil by reacting lovingly to that teenager when she is hard to understand.

I ask the Lord daily to help me to remember who my enemy really is. The Devil is my only enemy. This thought has helped me tremendously to not allow bitterness to enter my life. It has also helped me to keep myself in check as a wife and mother.

I am often amazed when I see conflicts between husbands and wives, parents and children, people and pastor, and Christians with each other that they cannot recognize how the Devil is trying to work havoc in their lives. Rather than fighting the real enemy, they lash out in bitterness toward their most beloved friends, and the Devil gets the victory.

I ask the Lord each day to bind the Devil and not allow him to have authority in my life and my loved ones' lives. I have seen tremendous victory in my relationships with others since I started this practice. I am not a "spooky" Christian, and the Devil gets little attention from me. But I know he is my enemy, and I know my God has power to make him helpless in my life and in my relationships.

3. Relationships always deteriorate when one partner is seeking to have his own needs met. A wife may say, "My husband doesn't meet my needs." As long as she keeps seeking to have her needs met, the Devil has victory in the relationship.

A child may say, "My parents don't treat me with respect. I want them to be proud of me." Again, the relationship will

crumble with this type of thinking.

In Ephesians 5, we see that the responsibility always comes before the reward. In other words, a wife must submit before she can have her needs met by her husband. A child must obey before she can earn the respect of her parents.

But the focus of the wife should not be having her needs met. Nor should the focus of the child be making her parents proud of her.

4. Relationships succeed when each partner gives the other what he himself wants. For example, if a wife doesn't feel like her husband is meeting a particular need in her life, she should check what that need is and decide to meet it in his life. Perhaps he doesn't give her the attention she needs to make her feel attractive and desirable. So she responds by telling him how attractive and desirable he is to her. I cannot say that I always respond as I should in this way. But when I do, it always works.

Children or even adults may long for their parents to meet their needs by treating them with respect or by being proud of them. The child should respond by treating her parent with the pride and respect with which she would like to be treated.

As long as a relationship runs by these philosophies and is bathed by the Word of God and prayer, it is destined to succeed over the Devil. However, when selfishness becomes our aim, the Devil is sure to destroy our relationships, thereby destroying our success as a Christian.

The Simple Life

"But I fear, lest by any means, as the serpent beguiled Eve through his subtilty, so your minds should be corrupted from the simplicity that is in Christ." (II Corinthians 11:3)

Often after my husband or I have finished counseling with someone about a marriage problem or some other type of problem, we comment about how complicated life can become. Yet, I don't believe God intended life to be complicated. The Bible says that *"God is not the author of confusion, but of peace, as in all churches of the saints."* (I Corinthians 14:33)

I often look at my own life and am amazed at how simple it has been. (I know you're probably saying, "Sure, a simple life for a simple mind.") I look at my life and realize that there have been some hard times. Yet sometimes because of the simplicity, the joy, and the love which I have experienced in my life, I forget that I have problems and hardships. The other day I was sympathizing with a friend of mine about some hardships in her life. My friend replied with, "Cindy, your problems have been bigger and harder than mine." I honestly had to stop and think about what problems she was referring to. You see, mine has been a simple life.

Again, I am not saying that the Christian life is not hard. My sisters and I often quote the saying, "Life is tough and then you die." That is hardly an uplifting comment, but it may seem accurate at times. However, I do not believe that life has to be complicated—hard maybe, but not complicated.

The Bible says that Eve's mind was corrupted from the simplicity which is in Christ. How so? It was complicated because Eve was beguiled by Satan. When God gave Eve a very simple command, Eve began to find excuse (with the Devil's help) as to why she did not need to follow God's simple command. When she did, life became complicated!

I believe the reason for my simple life stemmed from my following some simple commands which God has given. Most of the people I try to help who have complicated their lives have done it by making excuses as to why they are not required to obey God's simple commands. Let me give you a few examples.

A simple command: *"Wives, submit yourselves unto your own husbands, as unto the Lord." "Husbands, love your wives…"* Most, if not all, of the marriage problems my husband and I have helped with would not have been in existence if one or more of the parties involved had obeyed a simple command. Always where there is a marriage problem, there are excuses as to why God's simple commands for marriage do not need to be followed in their lives. I find in God's Word the commands, but I do not find the excuses.

Marriage may have to be hard. Some marriage partners may be hard to live with. All marriage partners are hard to live with sometimes! But marriage does not have to be complicated.

I simplified my life when I decided there would be no excuses. I would submit to my husband no matter what. Our marriage has been much simpler since. It has been hard since I made that decision, but never complicated.

I recently read some advice in a Christian marriage book which stated something like this: "If your husband is not meeting your needs, then try temporary separation. This will shake him and make the marriage stronger." My common sense tells me this may be a good idea, but to rely on my common sense is humanism or worse. I must follow God's simple command; not to make excuses.

Some excuses I have heard are: "My husband is not as easy to live with as yours is." "I think I married the wrong person." I find neither of these excuses in the Bible, only a simple command.

Another simple command is: *"Honour thy father and mother...."* Most of the rebellious and wayward teenagers and adults would think they are an exception to this simple command. They have a legitimate excuse for disobedience, or so they think. But the Bible gives no exceptions.

Years ago I made a simple decision to honor my parents. It was easy because they are wonderful and loving parents. However, my decision was firm. If they would have decided they hated me and if they would have told me so, it might have been hard to honor them. If they dishonored my name and the Lord's, it might have been hard to honor them. But it would not have complicated my life. My decision is firm. I will obey God's simple command.

Many simple principles which Brother Schaap and I have chosen to live by have simplified my life. For example, we have a principle that we will not leave a place of service unless God directly opens another door and without giving an authority in our lives veto power. (That does not mean control over every decision we make, but veto power over the major ones which will not only affect us, but our children. We do not wish to complicate their lives either.) We will not make a major decision when things are going wrong or when we are confused. All of these principles have simplified our lives and have, we believe, preserved us in God's will when times were hard. Allow me to give you some suggestions about how to live a simple life.

1. *"To day if ye will hear his voice, Harden not your heart."* (Psalm 95:7b, 8a) In other words, today, or any other day for that matter, if God speaks to your heart about one of His sim-

ple commands, don't make excuses. The Devil will give you plenty of excuses such as:

- "That preacher is too old. He doesn't understand me."
- "That speaker is too young. He couldn't possibly know the answer."
- "That person doesn't understand my situation."
- "That verse couldn't apply to me. It's just not practical in my life."

When you make excuses, your heart becomes hardened to the deceitfulness of sin, and you actually believe what you are doing is right.

2. Every time you hear or learn of one of God's simple commands, make a lifetime commitment to use it in your life. I am not saying that everyone who follows this advice will have a completely uncomplicated life. This chapter comes with no 30-day guarantee. It doesn't even come with a 30-minute guarantee. I am saying that to follow this advice will make your life at least some simpler. It will make the hard times less confusing and less complicated. It has for me!

I do not know what hardships the future holds for me. God may allow some hardships which will be more difficult than any experienced thus far. However when I look back, so far I see a simple life, full of some hardships, yet more full of peace and joy.

I do not know what hardships will have to be faced in my home or what heartaches will be shared by my husband and me. Yet I know from past experience that it does not have to be a complicated marriage. The hardest days can be filled with love. They have been thus far.

It is hard to rebuild a complicated life. It is much easier to protect a simple life. I want that kind of life for every reader. I'm thankful for my simple life and for the simplicity which is in Christ.

What I Have Learned About Friendship

It has often been said that "Friendship is a gift from God." This is something that I believe because it has been proven in my life several times.

When I was sixteen years old, I gave my life to the Lord. Though I was saved at the age of five, I was not completely sold out to the Lord until the beginning of my junior year of high school. God used the death of a friend Sharon to turn my life around. Sharon was almost killed in a car accident at the age of 16, and then died one year later in a fire. After Sharon's death and my surrender to the Lord, God sent a friend named Robyn. It was my desire to be Robyn's friend that helped me to straighten out my life.

Robyn was such a fun person that I strongly desired her friendship. Yet, she was such a fine Christian that I knew I was going to have to do some changing if I was going to fit into her crowd.

I did change, and Robyn and I became the best of friends. Part of the reason for my rebellion in high school had been a low self-esteem, and Robyn seemed to take it on as a personal challenge to build my confidence in myself. She was a constant encouragement to me. I have not seen Robyn in years, neither have I had much contact with her in any way, but I still think of her as my best girlfriend. She did something for me that no other friend has ever done. I did not seek her friendship. She was just there at a very important time in my life, and I have

no doubt that God placed her there.

Because of my identity as Dr. Jack Hyles' daughter, it has not always been easy for me to have close friends. Because of this, I have considered my family members to be my best friends. I have been especially close to my sister Linda through the years. Years ago Linda moved to Dallas, Texas, 1,000 miles away from where I live. Previous to that time, she had lived just around the corner from my house, and we had been truly best friends. Linda's move to Texas taught me a couple of things about friendship. First of all, it reminded me again that a friend is truly a gift of God.

Right before Linda moved, God sent a friend to sort of take her place in my life. A lady named Cathy Kimmel began to aggressively seek my friendship. I was the type of friend who had to be aggressively sought, and Cathy was persistent in her seeking, even though I often was unresponsive. Even now, Cathy and I are still very good friends. We do not spend a lot of time together, but we have made some wonderful memories through the years. Most of all, we have just tried to be there for each other when the other was in need. Cathy has the gift of helps. During any time of need, it seems that you look up, and there she is just happening to have the right thing to offer. I have not learned to be as helpful to Cathy as she is to me, but her example has inspired me to try. As I have already mentioned in the acknowledgments, Cathy helped to make this book a reality.

Linda's move also reminded me of the verse in Proverbs 18:24, *"A man that hath friends must shew himself friendly."* I am afraid that before Linda's move, I had not learned to be friendly. You see, I had always been close to my family. I had always had them as my best friends, and I had not felt the need to be a friend to anyone else. When Linda moved, I realized that it was important to be a friend even if, perhaps, you do not feel any tremendous need for friends. Since then, I have tried to obey Proverbs 18:24 by being friendly to everyone with whom I have come in contact.

I have learned that friends are something you should collect like shells. You should have as many different varieties as possible and take good care of all of them. I have not sought friends so that I might possess them, but rather that I might truly learn to be a friend. I have learned that a man cannot be measured by the size of his house or his paycheck but in the quantity of people whom he has befriended. I have learned that being a type of friend like a Robyn or like a Cathy Kimmel is not as easy as it looks. Because of this, I have prayed every day for several years that God would teach me to be a friend.

Being a good friend is like so many things in the Christian life. You cannot become one unless the Lord works through you and teaches you what friendship is all about. So many of the friendships that I have made have come from serving the Lord together. As the Lord works through me, it is natural that many special friendships are formed. Some of my dearest friends are people whom my husband and I have helped through tough marriage problems and other problems. I value these friendships like precious possessions.

Friendship Is Forever

The most important concept that I have learned about friendship is that it is forever. I have had friends who have become disloyal and critical of my dad and the ministry here. Many times I have felt a desire to lash out and to seek revenge. Each time the Lord has pricked my heart and reminded me that if I am truly someone's friend, then nothing can be said or done can change that fact. I have made a conscious decision that if I have ever felt that a person was my friend at any time in my life, then I would remain that person's friend forever. I do that by praying for her daily and most of all, by just recording in my mind that friendship never changes. If any friend should ever need me, I would want to be there for her regardless of the hurts she may have inflicted upon me. Though I would defend a hurting friend if it was my place to do so, I would never allow my love for another friend to be destroyed completely.

Lastly, I could never write an article on friendship without mentioning Christ's friendship to me. He has always been there when I needed Him, being a Friend and sending friends my way. He has loved me when I failed to show myself friendly and when I have hurt His friends. He has been committed to me in friendship even when I have failed Him. I value the word "friendship" and my very best Friend more and more as the years pass.

Please Read My Billboard!

Proverbs 14:1 says, *"Every wise woman buildeth her house; but the foolish plucketh it down with her hands."*

Ladies often come to me and present the particular problems they experience with their husbands or with their children. For example, a wife may say, "My husband never spends any time with the family," or "My husband doesn't pay our bills or give me any money," or "My husband doesn't show up for appointments."

A mother may say, "My children don't respect me," or "My children won't obey me."

I usually respond by asking, "Do you ever have any fun with your husband? Do you ever just really enjoy being together?"

Often she responds, "No, of course not, but that's not the problem. How can we have fun together when my husband doesn't give me any money? We need to fix that problem first."

I ask, "Do you and your husband ever laugh together?"

She answers, "Of course not. I don't laugh with my husband because he doesn't handle the money properly."

I inquire, "Do you ever brag on your husband? You know, do you ever tell him something you really like about him?"

She might reply, "Why would I brag on him? We have too many problems we are trying to work on in our marriage."

I then try to explain that you must build a relationship with a person before you begin to try to fix the problems in the relationship. To try to fix a relationship when no relationship has been built is as foolish as trying to fix the plumbing in a house before the foundation of the house has ever been laid. A lady must build a relationship with her husband and children before she can hope to fix any problems in any relationship. How then can a lady go about doing this?

1. Praise builds relationships. Evangelist Dennis Corle preached a sermon in Hyles-Anderson College chapel in which he pointed out that the Bible says that God inhabits praise. He said that if we are going to build a habitation for God, we should then praise Him. I began to relate this message to the home, and I realized that if God wants us to build Him a house through praise, He surely had praise in mind in Proverbs 14:1 where He told women to build their houses.

A woman who regularly praises her family is building a relationship with her loved ones. Each new compliment or loving thought which is expressed is making for a more solid relationship. Often women who regularly praise their family members find that problems take care of themselves. At other times, they discover that problems are solved smoothly because they are solved where a solid relationship has already been built.

I view my family members as having gas tanks which need to be filled each morning. I imagine that the gasoline (of self-confidence) has been drained during the night, and each morning I must start from the beginning in refueling the tank. Now as long as I have sufficiently fueled the tank, I expect my household to run smoothly. If the tank is running on empty or on the wrong fuel of bitter, unkind words, I find there arise problems which seem unsolvable. And they are unsolvable as long as I fail to build the relationship.

2. Memories build relationships. As a child, I had a regular baby sitter. She was a woman in her sixties named Louise Clifton, who passed away with a stroke. As I attended her funeral, I couldn't help remembering that Mrs. Clifton always had time. When I went to her house, she would usually pop some popcorn and pour us each a glass of 50/50 (one of the best soft drinks man has formulated, I might add). We would sit down and play games by the hour. When we tired of playing games, usually several hours later, we would either walk together to the corner store or to the park, or we would make supper.

Mrs. Clifton had a huge kitchen which was located, of all places, in her basement. As a child, I came home from Mrs. Clifton's house and told my parents that we didn't have a kitchen in the basement, so we didn't have "nothin'."

Besides my mother, Mrs. Clifton was the best cook in the world. Yet she let me "help" her make her huge breakfasts and suppers time and time again. Her kitchen was more like a playground to me. I have fond memories of Mrs. Clifton, and so do many other young adults and children in my church. My own children spent several days at her house, and their days with her were described exactly like those I experienced with her.

I also sat with Mrs. Clifton in church, and I had a problem with sitting still. I have always loved to wiggle in church. I especially loved to cross my legs and swing the top one as high as I could. Mrs. Clifton never lost patience with me in church. She never yelled or jerked me. She simply held her arm straight out down the row, and that was my signal to sit still—swinging leg and all. I always immediately obeyed "Aunt Louise" as I called her. I had, after all, such a close relationship built with this woman that I never considered not obeying. My memories of fun times with her caused me to want to obey.

2. Laughter builds relationships. My dad was a funny man. He had a great sense of humor. But as a father of children, he was more than a funny man. He was a silly man. I enjoyed my moments with my father very much. I know that is one reason why, during my most difficult teenage years, I did not rebel against him. I always wanted to please my father. We had few problems between us, and what problems we did have were easily and smoothly solved.

I can think of other things which would build a relationship, physical affection not being the least of these. Couples who are affectionate with one another will find that their problems are solved more easily.

Ladies, please let me encourage you to build and to strengthen your relationship with your husband before you try to correct a problem. In closing, allow me to use an illustration which so aptly got this point across to me.

When my son Kenny was little, he had trouble keeping his shoes tied. Because of this, we often tied his laces in what is called a double knot. (Most mothers of young children are very familiar with this practice.) One day Kenny was having trouble untying his double knot. "Mom," he said, "couldn't we just cut these shoe strings and buy new ones? This knot is just too hard to untie."

"Here, Kenny," I said, "let me try." In just a few seconds of patience, I untied what he had been about to cut, and I saved one perfectly good pair of shoe strings. Shortly thereafter, I saw a sign on the billboard of a printing business near our church which read, "Never cut that which can be untied."

Often in our relationships, we are prone to solve our problems by "cutting" rather than by "untying." We run to people we love with unkind words and threats in order to solve what we see as a problem in our relationship. Ladies, please learn with me a lesson from Kenny's untied shoes. Think of the people you love and of the people you try to influence. Then reflect on the eternal truth in Proverbs 14:1, *"Every wise woman buildeth her house; but the foolish plucketh it down with her hands."* And in closing, please read my billboard:

Never tear down those whom you can build.

P. S.   Don't cut yourself down when you see problems in your own Christian life. Just keep building your relationship with Jesus through the Bible and prayer. He can fix the problems easily and smoothly!

You Must Be God's Kid!

When I was a little girl, people often said to me, "Your mother is beautiful." Just as often, people said to me, "You don't look a thing like your mother." I must admit that I was disappointed a little bit that God did not make me tall, blonde, and beautiful like my mom.

Yet, I loved to hear the words, "You look just like your dad," and I did hear that statement made time and time again. "You have his piercing, brown eyes," people said, and I loved it.

When Jaclynn and Kenny were small, I once overheard a conversation between them that went something like this:

"*I* look like Dad. *You* look like Mom."

"No, *I* look like Dad, and *you* look like Mom."

"No, *you* look like Mom."

"No, *you* look like her."

My feelings were not really too hurt. It is pretty well understood in our house that we all love Dad the best. Putting it in slang, Dads are just a little "cooler" (as in fun, not in *cold*) than moms. There is something awfully "cool" about being like Dad.

Matthew 5:9 says, *"Blessed are the peacemakers: for they shall be called the children of God."* In the margin of my reference Bible, the word "resemble" is by Matthew 5:9. When we are peacemakers, we are able to actually resemble our Father.

In our house at 8232 Greenwood Avenue, my dad, Dr. Jack Hyles, was a peacemaker. When trouble or controversy arose, Dad did not rile me up; instead, he calmed me down.

I remember the gas crisis in the 1970's. An adult told some high school friends and me that the gas crisis probably meant our freedom in America would soon end. He really riled us up.

I went home and talked with Dad, and he calmed me down. Dad calmed my fears, my questions, and my controversies. Dad was a peacemaker in my life.

Nobody can rightly rile a crowd with their preaching like the men in my life, and I love that about them. But I know that I am truly blessed because my father and the father of my children are peacemakers.

I want to be a peacemaker. I don't want to walk into lives and "rile up" and upset folks. I want to bring peace to the lives of people I encounter.

I hate to admit this, but I once said to a girl, "I don't think 'so-and-so' likes me." I expected her to agree. But instead the girl repeated some kind thing the person had said about me and gently told me it could be just my imagination. Soon after, I was reading Proverbs 12:20 which says, *"Deceit is in the heart of them that imagine evil: but to the counsellors of peace is joy."* I pictured this girl's face, my peacemaker, and learned a valuable lesson.

A lot of the evil we think about is truly just imagined. We imagine people do not like us, or we imagine that someone looked at us funny. We imagine that someone is talking bad about us. We should recognize these thoughts as the Devil's attack, and we should refuse to imagine evil. If we don't know they don't like us, why imagine it? If someone truly doesn't like us, it usually doesn't hurt to go on believing he or she likes us.

The world is full of strife. The Devil is the one who puts it there. Let us not imagine evil or cause others to imagine evil. Instead, let us be counselors of peace. The Bible says that joy will follow.

If you hear someone say something bad about another person, don't repeat it. If you hear someone say something good about another person, run to that person and share it. Be a peacemaker.

I am thankful for a girl much younger than I who once was a peacemaker in my life. She gently pointed out that it was my imagination that some other person did not like me. This young girl changed my life permanently because she was a counselor of peace in my life.

I want to be a peacemaker because I want to look just like my Father—my Heavenly Father.

Living
on the Bright Side
As a Preacher's Wife

Making the Valley
a Well

In 1996, my husband was presented with many new responsibilities at Hyles-Anderson College. Though we both considered the new opportunities a special blessing, 1996 held many adjustments and questions for us, not to mention a very busy schedule. This busy schedule prevented me from writing for the *Christian Womanhood* paper as faithfully as I would have liked. The year 1996 was a year which held many questions for me as the wife of a leader.

I once again read through my mother's book, *Woman, the Assembler,* and I kept it on my night stand beside my bed to answer questions which arose. This book helped me tremendously, but I still had some questions which remained unanswered. I went to bookstores and searched through my library looking for books for the preacher's wife. My ever-helpful husband drove me to some bookstores, and we searched the shelves together. We were surprised at how little material there is available for the preacher's wife. We were thankful for my mother's book and wished that more leaders' wives would share their insights through the written word.

Many of us have questions that we wait for a specific person to answer. Sometimes we do not understand the answers thoroughly until we have read them several times from several different people. Then suddenly, a light turns on!

I searched through the Bible for the answers. As I read the Bible this year, I found more verses than ever before, telling me how much God loves me. I read verses that assured me that I could trust God. No matter how hard I searched, my questions remained unanswered. It was as if God were saying, "Cindy, I love you, and I am going to surround you in a special way with My love, but I am going to allow you to remain confused." God was very good to me in 1996, yet He seemed strangely silent.

"Cindy," my husband said, "you will find the answers to questions, and when you do, I want you to write about them. I want you to help other ladies through the adjustments they will face which are like the ones you are facing."

A verse that was especially dear to me in 1996 was Psalm 84:6a which says, *"Who passing through the valley of Baca made it a well...."* The word *Baca* means "weeping." I did a lot of weeping in 1996. I realize that in 1996 many others suffered in ways much worse than I, but I have learned to respect the depth of all valleys alike. In all valleys, the greatest sorrow is that God seems absent. Perhaps He is absent in not answering our prayer of healing or of sparing the life of a loved one. These are greater valleys than I experienced in 1996.

There is an old saying that goes, "If all of our troubles were hung on a line, you would take yours, and I would take mine." I would definitely choose my troubles over yours, but I walked through a valley in 1996.

In June of 1997, during an early morning walk through the woods in Holland, Michigan, God gave me some verses that were to me the answers to my questions. God and I are speaking again, and I can see the way to go as far as my questions are concerned.

It is said that the best teachers are the ones who teach what they just learned themselves. I hope that is true because for the next several chapters, I am going to take on my husband's challenge. I am going to share with you what God shared with me during that time. The purpose of this chapter is just to intro-

duce you to the forthcoming ones.

By now you are probably wondering what my questions were in 1996. I will not tell you my specific questions. I am not ready to do that; I may never be ready. However, I *am* going to share with you some problems that resulted because of those questions and how God has helped me to begin to conquer them. For now, let me just encourage you to keep on seeking the Lord with your questions, and don't be afraid to ask for the help of others. I did that, too. I was determined that I would not alienate myself from others during my valley time. Part of my valley I walked with my parents and my in-laws and, of course, my husband was there for me all the way during an extremely busy and pressured time of his life. They all are the best, and I thank them.

If you have found some specific answers as a preacher's wife or just as a Christian in general, I beseech you to find a way to share them with others. They need you; I need you! So, I have set out to start the task of building a well. In case there are others who will walk through my particular valley someday, they will find a refreshment to quench their thirsty souls and make it safely to the other side. Please share this journey with me.

When You Feel Insignificant or Unworthy

"As ye have therefore received Christ Jesus the Lord, so walk ye in him: Rooted and built up in him, and stablished in the faith, as ye have been taught, abounding therein with thanksgiving. For in him dwelleth all the fulness of the Godhead bodily. And ye are complete in him." (Colossians 2:6, 7, 9, 10a)

Problem #1
A preacher's wife often feels insignificant and unworthy.

Solution: A preacher's wife should find her significance in her walk with God. "As ye have therefore received Christ Jesus the Lord, so walk ye in him: Rooted and built up in him." (Colossians 2:6, 7a)

I have said before in my writings and in my teachings that I am not a perfectionist. Lately, I have realized that this is not the whole truth. I am not a perfectionist in all of my work. I do not care if my house is not perfectly clean. I am not the person to ask to make a sign if that sign needs to be perfect. I cannot tell if the letters are perfectly straight, and I do not care if they are perfectly straight. I am not a perfectionist in all things. There is only one thing that I expect to be perfect—me!

Everyone knows that a preacher's wife is supposed to be perfect. She should be a wonderful wife who attends all the church functions, and of course, she should also have an immaculate house. She should host parties and take time to train her children. She should be a wonderful cook, and yet she should be fit and trim in her figure. She should be beautiful, but not at all vain. She should be a great speaker, but she should not be outspoken.

I'm afraid that I sometimes feel unable to live up to such a standard, how about you? Yet I'm afraid that is a standard that some preachers' wives set for themselves. My standard for myself has been just about that ridiculous at times. This standard has left me feeling somewhat unworthy and insignificant as a preacher's daughter and wife at times. You see, nobody is perfect, and neither am I. In fact, in some ways I may fall quite short of what an ideal preacher's wife should be. Let me give you an example.

I am afraid of the "bogey man." Now everyone knows that a good preacher's wife should not be afraid to stay at home alone at night, but I am (or at least I was). In fact, when my husband first started traveling and preaching, I bundled up my two small children and headed to my parents' house to spend the night. I remember walking into their house one evening, looking my dad in the eye and saying, "I'm no Mrs. John R. Rice."

Ever my encourager, my father responded, "You may be like Mrs. John R. Rice when she was 24."

In recent years, I have conquered my fear of being alone, or shall I say, God took it away after much prayer. Yet one night, after several years of not being afraid, I awoke in the middle of the night horrified. I heard a sound in the basement, and I just knew it was a burglar. I called my parents, and then I called the police. The police came and found nothing, then left. After they left, I found the culprit, and we met face to face!

My burglar was a mouse chewing a cracker wrapper under my family room couch! What kind of a preacher's wife would be afraid of a mouse? How can I stand at the martyr's stake, or when my husband needs me to, when the rattling of a cracker wrapper may send me into orbit? (In fact, what kind of preacher's wife would have a cracker wrapper under her family room couch in the first place?)

These were my thoughts the morning after my episode with the police. They probably have you laughing now as they do me, but I was not laughing then. I was disappointed with myself. I thought I had overcome my problem, and now years later, I was acting more like a child than a seasoned preacher's wife. This weakness and others often have me feeling insignificant and unworthy to be the wife of a leader. Other leaders' wives surely do not struggle with such problems...or do they?

Jesus tells me, however, that I am not to find my significance in myself, but rather in my walk with Him. Colossians 2:7 tells us that we are to be "rooted" in Christ. Christ is to be the very foundation of our innermost feelings about ourselves. This verse also tells us that we are to be "built up" in Christ. Not only should our walk with Christ be that which establishes our feelings about ourselves, but our walk with Him should be that which is most reflected in our public image.

Nobody is perfect, but everyone can seek God and get to know Him. When a lady becomes a preacher's wife, her first priority should be to develop a walk with Christ. When she feels insignificant and tempted to compare herself with some other lady in the church, she should remember that nobody is perfect. God does not expect the preacher's wife to be more perfect than anyone else. He expects her to walk with Him. The preacher's wife who is walking with God is as unworthy as any other woman to be used of God. When she is rooted and built up in her walk with Christ, she develops a special significance to God as He is able to work through her.

So you see, I have a lot of weaknesses—some that have left

me with the problem of feeling unworthy and insignificant at times, especially as my husband's ministry has grown. Yet I have never felt shy about saying to others, "Follow me as I follow Christ." Why? Because in spite of all of my weaknesses, I am seeking the One Who makes just the perfect preacher's wife.

Preachers' wives, I love you like I have never loved you before. Please do not compare yourself with others and feel that you are lacking. Just get to know your God and let Him work through you. Find your significance in Him. He thinks you are wonderfully special. And remember this, nobody is perfect...except Him!

When You Feel Afraid

"*As* *ye have therefore received Christ Jesus the Lord, so walk ye in him: Rooted and built up in him, and stablished in the faith, as ye have been taught, abounding therein with thanksgiving. For in him dwelleth all the fulness of the Godhead bodily. And ye are complete in him.*" (Colossians 2:6, 7, 9, 10a)

Problem #2
A preacher's wife often feels afraid.

Solution: A preacher's wife should be "*stablished in the faith.*"

I love flowers! I guess I inherited this love from my mother. Every spring Mom and I discuss on the telephone what we have bought and planted in our yards. Actually, I try to keep myself away from nurseries in the spring because I find myself wanting to buy some of every seed and plant.

I plant around 100 annuals every spring. I also have many perennial flowers. My favorite perennial flower is the black-eyed Susan. Each summer the hardy black-eyed Susans bloom and multiply in my garden. Even though I fail to cover them and protect them from the winter elements, they still come back in fuller fashion each year than they did the year before.

One year on our anniversary, my husband bought me five rose bushes. These rose bushes are very delicate. They must be pruned a few times a year. They need fertilizer and bug protection more than the black-eyed Susans do. In the fall of the year, I cover my roses with a cone-shaped protector. They are too precious to be exposed to the harsh, cold winter weather.

A preacher's wife should not treat herself like the hardy flower. Rather, she should treat herself like the more precious and delicate rose. A preacher's wife is more like the exotic, tropical plant which must be kept in a greenhouse in a perfect climate, or else it will soon die.

As a preacher's wife, my job is a delicate one. I am here to encourage my preacher husband. I am not a very big person, nor am I a very strong person. In fact, fear is a weakness with which I struggle in my life.

I was the confidanté and the encourager of the man who handled all of the discipline problems of our college. No, my husband did not tell me all of the discipline problems at the college, but we did sometimes discuss his feelings when he had a particularly difficult day of discipline.

I was the spirit-lifter of one of the men who carried on his shoulders the spirit-lifting of all the students, staff, and faculty at Hyles-Anderson College.

Now I am the wife of the pastor of the "World's Largest Sunday School." He is a man who carries, perhaps, a bigger load than any human has ever carried. He carries a load which is larger and heavier than any of us could begin to understand. Sometimes the things my husband faces and the problems of our society frighten me. Sometimes the future frightens me. How can a fearful woman like I am be a help to such important people with such important tasks?

Easy! I follow God's Word when it tells me "*stablish*" (which means *strengthen*) myself in the faith. I am learning to handle my fear by treating myself like that delicate rose about which I was talking. The following are ways I strengthen myself.

1. I protect myself from the harsh, cold elements of the world. I made a decision several years ago that I would not watch television. One of the reasons for that decision is that television and its negative programs make me afraid.

I do not watch the news. Why? Because the television news is full of negative reports we do not need to know. For example, we do not need to know who was raped last week. Nor do we need to know what public figure is in trouble morally.

The newspaper is also full of unnecessary reporting. I am careful of what I read in the newspaper, and I catch most of my news by way of radio because it tends to be more concise. I am also careful, however, about what kind of and how much radio I hear.

2. I protect myself from the winter winds of negativity. I stay away from negative people. *I do not go through my hus-band's papers on his desk.* If the Lord sends a person my way whom I can help, I help her. I do not look for trouble, neither do I meddle in other people's strife.

3. Most importantly of all, I protect myself from myself. I have found that the thing that can harm my spirit more than anything and cause me to be afraid the most is my own self.

I protect myself from my own criticism. As soon as I notice myself thinking one tiny critical thought, I confess it to the Lord as sin and find something positive to occupy my mind. Let me share an example of a tiny critical thought: "Bless her heart, she's gained weight."

I used to think that if I said "bless her heart" first, I was almost doing her a favor by criticizing her. Now I am learning how just one critical statement can blossom into a negative, fearful attitude, which can lead to a negative family and a neg-ative day. This leads to my preacher husband having a wife who cannot meet his needs.

I protect myself from my own negative thinking. When I begin to fear or worry in my mind, I begin immediately to occu-py my mind with positive thinking.

4. I strengthen myself with faith. Some ways I do this each day are as follows:

a. I listen to sermon tapes instead of watching television.

b. I listen to praise music instead of listening to contemporary or melancholy Christian music.

c. I pray while I work instead of criticizing.

d. I sing while I work instead of worrying.

e. I speak my blessings out loud to God instead of griping.

f. I stop between tasks to read special Bible verses instead of reading another chapter in a novel.

g. I do something for someone else or go soul winning instead of going on a shopping binge.

h. I exercise instead of eating a hot fudge sundae.

i. I go outdoors instead of sitting in front of the television.

j. I nap when I need to, rather than driving myself to exhaustion.

My dad has taught us that Song of Solomon says that a wife is to be a garden for her husband's enjoyment. Every preacher's wife needs to realize that she is not a garden of wild flowers which needs very little tending. She is not a garden of hardy annuals like petunias or marigolds. She is a rare, sensitive and beautiful garden of roses or tropical flowers. She must tend to herself with care!

She is not to protect herself like the garden in the backyard; she is to protect herself like the garden at the White House. For you see, someone much more important than the President of the United States seeks solace in her garden. She gets to be the solace of a man of God!

Preacher's wife, protect yourself from fear. You can face the future and the problems of your husband's ministry one day at a time. You do this by strengthening yourself in the faith. And remember, Preacher's wife, to God and to me you are more beautiful than any flower that has ever bloomed.

Overcoming Self-Pity

"*As ye have therefore received Christ Jesus the Lord, so walk ye in him: Rooted and built up in him, and stablished in the faith, as ye have been taught, abounding therein with thanksgiving. For in him dwelleth all the fulness of the Godhead bodily. And ye are complete in him.*" (Colossians 2:6, 7, 9, 10a)

Problem #3
A preacher's wife sometimes feels self-pity.

Solution: A preacher's wife should be "*abounding therein with thanksgiving.*"

"How are you doing?" I asked Jean Petsch. At that time Jean was on my husband's staff as Admissions Secretary at Hyles-Anderson College.

"Wonderful!" Jean replied. "I'm getting married in 87 days."

Amused, I continued down the college hallway, hoping that Jean would feel that way, not only throughout her entire engagement, but also during all the years of her marriage. Jean's attitude toward her fiancé Walter definitely reminded me of the phrase in Colossians 2 which says "*abounding therein with thanksgiving.*" She possessed an overflowing, grateful spirit as she looked forward to her wedding day.

I enjoy working with the girls at Hyles-Anderson College for that very reason. I get to teach them and watch them as they fall in love, become engaged, and get married. My goal as a teacher at the college is to do my part to see that every girl whom God desires to be a preacher's wife becomes one. Rarely do I watch an engaged girl look forward to her wedding without that sparkle in her eye which tells me that she is *"abounding therein with thanksgiving."*

Yet it sometimes seems to be just about as rare to find a wife of several years who exudes with that same enthusiasm. As a preacher's wife, I must admit, there have been times when my thanksgiving for my husband was lacking and was instead replaced with self-pity. I have said to myself things such as the following:

• "Her husband goes to work at 9:00 a.m. and comes home at 5:00 p.m. and spends the whole evening at home. My husband often works evenings and is even 'on call' during his evening hours at home. Poor me!"

• "Her husband is available on weekends to manicure the lawn and fix what needs to be fixed. My husband barely finds time to care for himself when he is at home. (I must say here that he does not neglect me and our children, and he never has.) Uh-oh! That statement almost ruined my pity party— poor me!"

• "Her husband doesn't travel. Mine takes at least one trip every two weeks. When he's gone, it never fails that the dog barks through the night, the house creaks, and I awake missing my bed partner. Poor me!"

• "Worse yet, it seems that I share my husband, his time, and our money with thousands of people whenever they have a need. Poor, poor, poor, poor me!"

All of these are very exaggerated statements I sometimes make to myself at my pity party. Fortunately, the Holy Spirit directs my attention at times like this to verses such as Colossians 2:7, and I am reminded that the antidote to self-pity is thanksgiving.

During a preaching trip my husband took, I was invited to dinner with a friend, a lady in her early thirties who had lost her husband of eight years. She was also the mother of four children, all under the age of six.

During our dinner, she shared about her faith in God and her appreciation for the eight years He had given her with her husband. Though this friend is obviously very lonely, she did not display self-pity to me. Rather she praised her husband for being a great husband and for giving her a wonderful marriage and four precious children. "I would rather have been married to my husband for eight years than to anyone else for a lifetime."

At the funeral home, my friend hugged our 16-year-old daughter Jaclynn and said, "I hope God gives you a husband as wonderful as mine was."

I left my dinner with my widowed friend not having seen my husband for 48 hours and knowing that I would not see him again for another 24. Yet, I was not feeling sorry for myself. In fact, I felt rather ashamed, and I felt thankful.

When I am tempted to feel the self-pity that invades the life of a preacher's wife, I think of people like this widow, and I decide to "abound with thanksgiving."

My husband and I began to count the days to our wedding when there were still over 500 left. During those days, I decided that I would always stay excited about my husband—even if the rest of the world found me to seem as immature as a starry-eyed bride-to-be. My husband and I have strived for this for every year of our marriage, and I do not regret it. I would rather have my preacher husband with me part of the time than any other husband all of the time!

Not long after this luncheon, I passed Jean Petsch in the hall at the college. Her name is now Mrs. Walter Santos. "How are you doing, Jean?" I asked again.

"Wonderful!" she again replied, "and it's because of whom I married."

I was proud and happy for Jean that she was still excited about her new husband. But, Jean, I have you beat—you see, I am still very excited and thankful for my husband after having had the privilege of being his wife since June 1, 1979! May every preacher's wife combat the problem of self-pity by *"abounding therein with thanksgiving."*

Triumphing Over Loneliness and Insecurity

"*As* ye have therefore received Christ Jesus the Lord, so walk ye in him: Rooted and built up in him, and stablished in the faith, as ye have been taught, abounding therein with thanksgiving. For in him dwelleth all the fulness of the Godhead bodily. And ye are complete in him…" (Colossians 2:6, 7, 9, 10a)

Problem #4: A preacher's wife often feels lonely and insecure.

Solution: A preacher's wife should find her security in Christ. "*And ye are complete in him….*" (Colossians 2:10a)

As the youngest daughter of an extremely busy pastor and wife, I must admit that I came into marriage as a very independent person. Though my parents always took time for me and we were very close, their busy schedule as well as my "loner" type of nature had made me a very independent soul.

During the early years of my marriage, my husband showed me how I needed to be more dependent upon him. I really worked to make our marriage a priority in life and to depend upon my husband more. I put aside many of my own personal ambitions and allowed my life to revolve around my husband's dreams. Brother Schaap and his ministry became my ministry. As a result, Brother Schaap and I became extremely close and family-oriented, and I felt very secure. I suppose you could say that I found my security in my husband.

A couple of years into our marriage, God blessed Brother Schaap and me with a daughter Jaclynn. About the time of Jaclynn's first birthday, I recall looking at her and feeling completely amazed at how much her little life had won my heart. Three and a half years later, God blessed our home again with a son Kenny. As I lived through the busy years of rearing small children, I felt for the first time that I had found where I really belonged. Being a wife and a mother seemed to definitely be my niche. To this day, I have never felt like I am in my element any more than when I am at home simply being a wife and a mother. Having a family positively made this loner type of person feel secure. *"God setteth the solitary in families."* (Psalm 68:6) As my family grew, I became more and more dependent upon them to meet my needs. I believed I was doing the right thing, and my husband was pleased.

Then my life began to change as life so often does. My children entered junior high and then high school. More and more they stayed late at school and became involved in extra-curricular activities. To the career-oriented woman, this would have been a relief, but to me, it was lonely. I missed my children very much. A gradual shift in my feeling of security began to take place, though I did not recognize it all at once.

Soon after my oldest child entered high school, my husband's responsibilities at Hyles-Anderson College increased. Though his responsibilities had increased yearly since Brother Schaap was hired in 1978, our lives changed drastically when he became the vice president of Hyles-Anderson College in 1996. Brother Schaap loved his job, and I sensed almost immediately that he was happier than he had been in a long time. Though my husband never neglected his family, he began to leave earlier to go to the college, and he also stayed later. I was happy for my husband; his success was the most important thing in the world to me. Yet my feeling of insecurity grew stronger.

I must admit that on my weaker days, I felt that my whole family had betrayed me. I had made them my life, and now I felt abandoned. I do not tell you this to receive any pity, but rather because I promised myself during those lonely days that I would use whatever I was going through to help others some-day—even if it meant admitting my own weakness.

My husband knew that I was struggling deeply. He sat me down and admonished me that I needed to be more independent. Being the great Christian that I am, this was my response: "Humph! (or something like that) My husband is the one who wanted me to become dependent; now he is telling me I need to be more independent."

I became even more confused as the months passed when Brother Schaap told me he wanted me to be more independent when he was away from home and more dependent when he was home. How in the world was I to maintain a tough, strong spirit when my husband was away and then become sweet, gentle, and dependent when he walked in the door? I asked myself, "Couldn't my husband just change jobs?"

My answer to myself came quickly. "No, he can't. My husband is a preacher; I am a preacher's wife. My husband does not belong to me; he belongs to God. My husband doesn't need to change; I must change."

Then one day in June of 1997, I found the verse in Colossians which says, *"And ye are complete in him…"* God used that verse to point out that in Him I could be all my husband needed me to be. I could be the tough, strong wife when my husband was away, and I could be the sweet, dependent wife when my husband walked through the door.

I also learned that I could be secure as my children continued to grow and build their own lives. You see, they do not belong to me either. They are God's to take them and use them wherever He wants them.

Proverbs 3:26a says, *"For the LORD shall be thy confidence."* As time passes, I am realizing more and more that the Lord is to be my security, and nothing or no one else can take His place. As I find my security in Christ, I am more and more confident that I can be whatever my loved ones need for me to be. And I am adequate to help my husband accomplish any task, whether it be great or small.

So I write to all of the ladies who find themselves in a similar phase of life such as the one I have shared with you. And I especially write to the preachers' wives who, in their own unique way, must realize that their husband is not theirs to be their sole source of security. I ask you to remember this: You can live a full and confident life as you walk with Christ and serve Him by serving others. And Christ can make you complete enough to accomplish any task that He or your preacher husband needs you to accomplish. Never forget it! The Lord is your confidence, *"and ye are complete in him."*

Practical Solutions for the Problem of Loneliness

In the last chapter of this section, I shared with you a phase I went through in my life and the resulting loneliness. Here I want to give some practical solutions I have found for overcoming that loneliness.

1. Develop a closer walk with Christ. A wife and mother who finds herself often alone will find she is able to do more Bible study, Bible memory, and praying than she did in the past. This walk with Christ will make her a more confident person as she develops the independence necessary to conquer loneliness.

2. Don't ask your husband to adapt to your schedule; you adapt to his. As my husband's responsibilities have increased in his ministry, I have literally run after him. In other words, I have changed my schedule and have sought for creative ways to be with him. A few evenings when Brother Schaap was too busy to come home for dinner, I packed a picnic lunch, and our family ate dinner with him by the lake at the college.

I also became more involved in the college myself as my husband became busier. I took advantage of the extra time to teach some new classes and to become more involved in my husband's ministry.

3. Do try to live by schedule as much as possible. It is true that schedule brings security. Preachers' families are often insecure because they fail to live by a schedule. When my husband got busier, we tried even harder to live by schedule. For example, most evenings when my husband had to work late, he came home for dinner promptly at 5:30 p.m. When my husband first became vice president of the college, he and I put it in our schedules to take a walk every evening after dinner while our children did the dishes. After our walk, he would return to work.

4. As your children grow, you must stop making them adapt to your schedule, and you must learn to adapt to theirs. When our children were involved in church and school activities, I stopped whining and learned to live by this philosophy: "If you can't beat 'em, join 'em." I attended almost all of my son's sports events and my daughter's cheerleading events and so forth. As our children have grown, that confidence that I have done all I can to enjoy them has enhanced my ability to let go of them to the degree that the Lord wants me to let go. I believe many parents refuse to let go of their children properly because they are filled with regret for neglecting to enjoy their children properly when they were younger.

5. Replace lost time with your family with time spent doing for others. When our children were small and my husband was less busy, I went soul winning, and I tried to live for others. But I must admit that it was hard. I was busy training my children which I felt was a higher priority. As my family has grown and gotten busier, I have "comforted" myself by doing more for others.

6. Replace lost time with your family by nurturing friendships. I chose not to socialize much when my children were small, and this is a decision I do not regret. However, as my family has gotten busier, I have learned to value more the friendship of other women. It is especially good for a preacher's wife to find another preacher's wife with a similar situation so they can encourage each other.

As your family becomes busier and you have more time for friends, be careful that you don't become a gossip. It is best to spend time doing something with friends. Even then you must guard your conversation. Also, be careful if you spend time with friends whose husbands are not in the ministry. Be sure you do not compare your husband's schedule with their husband's schedule and begin to indulge in self-pity.

7. Spend more time outdoors. I have always found great comfort in being outdoors, especially during the busiest seasons of my husband's life. During nice weather, I walk two miles a day and pray. I eat meals while outdoors and read my Bible while outside. As my husband and family have gotten busier, I have found more time to take care of myself physically.

8. Develop a new interest or hobby. When I left the nest and got married, my mother took up several new hobbies. She took up oil painting and also began to teach and to write more.

In conclusion, allow me to express a warning. As your husband becomes busier, be sure that you replace his time mostly with other relationships and not with other things. Resist the temptation to become a hermit, though that does sound good to the watched preacher's wife at times.

Also, resist the temptation to replace your husband's time with the accumulation of things. When your husband cannot be your security, do not try to find security in materialism. Remember, life is people. As Mrs. Marlene Evans often said, "Love people and like things. Don't love things and like people." Handle your loneliness mainly by walking with Christ and by reaching out to others who are lonely also.

Tips for the Lonely Preacher's Wife

Like many other young girls, I dreamed of getting married from a very young age. Even though I had been a pastor's daughter all of my life and felt God had called me to marry a preacher, I still dreamed of having a husband who went to work at 9:00 a.m. and arrived home by 5:00 p.m. so that we could enjoy our family life together. I dreamed of having a husband by my side to unscrew the lids on pickle jars, etc.

When my husband and I had been married a few years, he began to receive invitations to preach out of town. I was aware that my husband was a wonderful preacher, and, of course, I felt flattered that other churches across the country wanted to have him come to preach at their churches. Yet, I dreaded the separations and experienced great loneliness when my husband began to travel.

I remember thinking when my husband first began to travel that all of my loneliness would subside when my husband finally arrived home. Yet, so often just the opposite took place. Instead of feeling my burden lifting and greeting my husband cheerfully when he walked in the door, I continued to feel melancholy and was not very much fun to be around. I found it difficult to enjoy the results of his meetings.

After this pattern had continued for some time, I knew that some changes needed to take place. I realized that if my attitude did not change, one of two things would happen. I would either cause my husband to quit his preaching ministry, or I would have a nervous breakdown. (Maybe not literally, but I think you know what I mean.)

The next trip my husband took, I did three different things which changed my attitude about loneliness and has caused my attitude to be different ever since.

- I spent extra time in Bible reading and prayer.
- I fasted for my husband's meeting. (I did not share this with anyone at the time, but I decided to share it with you now because I think it will be a help.)
- I planned a surprise for my husband. I believe that particular surprise was a batch of homemade cookies prepared for him when he walked in the door.

I will never forget the new excitement I felt when he returned and told me that 63 young people had surrendered to full-time Christian work. I felt that I had a part. I have met several of those young people at Hyles-Anderson College where they are studying for the ministry. I learned several things then and since then that have helped me through loneliness. Let me share them with you now.

1. Most importantly, I learned never to seek my joy from people, places, things, or my husband in particular. I learned to always seek my joy in the Lord. Psalm 37:4 challenges me to find my joy in the Lord. *"Delight thyself also in the LORD; and he shall give thee the desires of thine heart."*

There is not a wife in existence who has a husband who can be her joy. When a wife leans on her husband for her joy, she ceases to become attractive and challenging to him. Instead, she becomes a burden. Marriage is not for obtaining joy. Rather, it is for sharing a joy that you already possess. That joy can only be cultivated through a close relationship with the Lord.

The wise preacher's wife will turn to the Lord in Bible reading and prayer when she feels the pain of loneliness.

2. I learned to invest what I could in my husband's ministry at all times. I am more involved in some aspects of my husband's ministry than others. My husband and I have decided that there are some areas of his ministry where it is best that I not be extremely involved. Still, if I do not invest some part of my time to those areas of ministry which cause separation, I will feel left out and lonely. Prayer and fasting are just two good examples of how a wife can invest her time at those times when she is separated from her husband. Sending a thoughtful gift to the pastor's wife or to someone to whom your husband will be ministering is also a good idea.

3. I learned to handle loneliness by doing things for my husband and others. I don't know about you, but when I have a surprise for someone, I just can't be depressed. I get a sheepish grin on my face and can hardly control my enthusiasm when I have planned a surprise.

4. I learned to find great enjoyment in little things. When my sisters and I lived at home, we used to tease my mother about how excited she could get about little things. My mom could sit down with a cup of coffee and a good book and act like the greatest thing was about to happen. My sisters and I often joked that it didn't take much to make mom happy. Now I realize that my mother taught me a great lesson. Preachers' wives who are at home alone a lot (or home alone with several children) must learn to find enjoyment in the little things.

5. I learned to be tough and creative. I'm still working on the toughness, of course, but I did learn not to sit around feeling sorry for myself when I felt lonely. I think my children could vouch for the fact that when things get dull around my house, I plan some kind of adventure. I sometimes think that what preachers' wives need most to keep from burning out is simply some creativity.

Please allow me to share with you some ideas of ways to use your hubby's out-of-town time creatively.

- Plan a party for your Sunday school class. Your husband will appreciate your having those giggling girls over while he was gone.

- Invite a former Sunday school class member or bus kid over to spend the night. I have also invited college girls to spend the night during these times.

- Plan something special for your children. One autumn when my husband's schedule was particularly busy, I took my children to a special place on a regular basis. I told them that it was our secret place where we could go when we missed Daddy.

- Plan something special for yourself. My husband is one of those unusual people who rarely gets a taste for junk food. Because of this, we eat healthful food in our house most of the time. However, when the cat's away…we buy one extremely indulgent snack, and my children and I enjoy!

- Plan a surprise for your husband when he returns. It may be a welcome banner, a card with a sweet note, or some home-baked goodies. (My husband can stand home-baked junk food!) Use your imagination, but this should be the culmination of every trip.

- Talk a lot about daddy when he is away so that the children never get the idea that you are bitter about his absence. Your children do not need to feel that daddy is an unnecessary person in the home.

- Learn to switch from being independent to dependent when your husband returns home. A preacher's wife must be independently dependent. She must unscrew her own pickle jar lids without complaining one day and then remember to appreciate his help the next day.

- Don't depend too heavily on any other one man while your husband is out of town. Perhaps a man will volunteer to help from time to time. I don't know where my mother would have been without such volunteer help. Yet she never depended heavily on any one person through all of her years as a pastor's wife. She has had to depend on the Lord. How fortunate!

• Don't complain about your husband's absence to others. It is both unwise and unkind to say things such as, "I'm sorry about my yard. My husband just never gets around to doing it." Or, "I haven't seen my husband in weeks. I think I'll introduce myself to him next time I see him." I think we have all said such things teasingly, but if a bitter spirit exists, the message will come across to others loud and clear. Let's not put down our husbands in this way.

• When at times the loneliness becomes overwhelming, seek help from a counselor. I believe some marriages end when the problem was merely loneliness and could have been cured if the wife had sought some help before she did anything stupid. It would probably be wise to decide whom you would go to for advice before the person is needed. (A pastor or pastor's wife, etc., would be a good idea. It probably should not be a peer.)

In closing, I guess the cure for loneliness that comes to anybody's wife could be summarized in this well-used outline.

J—Jesus—When you're lonely, spend some extra time with Him.

O—Others—When you're lonely, do something for your husband and for others.

Y—Yourself—Do some little bitty thing for yourself and enjoy it as if it were something outstanding!

Most of our preacher husbands are good to include us in their ministries when it is possible. We get to be their partners in the ministry. They are also good to care for the needs at home when they can. Yet there will be frustrating and lonely times for a preacher's wife. Let's remember that it is a privilege to be the wife of a full-time Christian worker. Let's also remember that loneliness is a great opportunity to find our joy in the Lord. He always satisfies.

Conquering Giants—
A Lesson for the Pastor's Wife

Twelve spies were sent to spy in Canaan. Ten came back weak in faith, and they discouraged God's people. The "ministry" of conquering Canaan seemed too big for them. It was a "giant" of a task, and they felt overwhelmed by it. God was angry and disappointed; I think not only because these spies lacked faith, but also because they discouraged God's people. The Bible says that after the children of Israel heard the report of the ten spies, they cried, wept, and complained.

But two men, Joshua and Caleb, had a completely different spirit. The Bible implies that these men's attitudes about God's will for their lives were as different as night and day from the rest of the men. Because of this, these two were chosen to go into the land of Canaan, and the other men were left out. Not only did Joshua and Caleb profit because of their positive spirits, but so also did their families.

In this story, we can find many lessons that will help all of us who are wives and mothers, and even more so perhaps, those of us who are preachers' wives.

"The land, which we passed through to search it, is an exceeding good land. If the LORD delight in us, then he will bring us into this land, and give it us; a land which floweth with milk and honey. Only rebel not ye against the LORD, neither fear ye the people of the land; for they are bread for us: their defence is departed from them, and the LORD is with us: fear them not." (Numbers 14:7b-9)

1. Don't rebel against God's will for your life. God asked me to do something unusual in 2001. God asked me to support my husband as he took on the mission of pastoring the First Baptist Church of Hammond. It was, to a simple girl like me, a "giant" task to be the pastor's wife of such a large church. The task seemed overwhelming when I realized that I was being called on to share my husband and to comfort so many people when I myself was grieving the loss of my father.

Such a task could have caused rebellion. I felt the tug of rebellion in my heart very briefly in those months. I was tempted to shout to my husband, "This task is too big for us," or "This is not fair."

But then I remembered how God hates it when we discourage His people; so instead, each morning I told the Lord that I was submitting to His will for my life—all day long. (In situations like mine, you learn to live life one day at a time.) Pastors' wives, let me encourage you to tell the Lord each morning that you are submitting to His will. Take life one day at a time.

2. Don't fear the people. Guess what I discovered when my husband became the pastor of our church? I discovered that there are a lot of people in this church. I knew there were a lot of people when I was the pastor's daughter, but somehow those people can seem bigger than life now that I am the pastor's wife. They sometimes even seem like "giants." (No, I am not implying the people in our church are overweight!)

If a pastor's wife is not careful, she can become bogged down with the responsibilities of her husband, and she can begin to fear the people. They can be intimidating, and she can resent them.

The antidote is the love of Christ. *"There is no fear in love; but perfect love casteth out fear."* (I John 4:18a) God knew what He was doing when He led me to do a Bible study on love just months before my father's death. He was preparing me to love the people of First Baptist Church. When you love someone, you get busy helping that person, forgetting about her reactions or the consequences.

It is just as a mother tends to a sick child, not thinking about the labor or even whether the child is contagious. The mother loves the child with a God-given love. She has no fear. She just wants to be involved in helping the child in any way she can.

I strongly advise every pastor's wife to do a Bible study on love. Grow in love with the people and do not watch their every reaction. Believe the best about them and find as many ways as you can to help them. I know that a pastor's wife first has a responsibility to her husband, but sometimes a pastor's wife who is too uninvolved with the people develops a spirit which is discouraging to her husband.

It has been a privilege to comfort the church people at the same time I am grieving my father. The very act of comforting them has caused my husband and me to love them more. In return, they have comforted us so graciously, and we feel they love us more. My dad was so afraid the people of our church would not be loved when he was gone, but God has had a wonderful plan.

3. Remember, God is with us. Some time ago, just the very thought that the presence of God is with me became overwhelming to me. Though my husband still takes time for me, it is so comforting to feel the presence of God and to know that He will never leave me. Each morning I ask God to speak to me and to show Himself to me that day. Then I look for evidence of God's presence. Sometimes He shows Himself to me in small ways. Sometimes He shows Himself to me in truly miraculous ways. But I see evidence of God's presence in beautiful ways every day. As I watch Him, it is hard to be afraid of the "giants" that we face in our ministry. Pastors' wives, the answer to your discouragement is a consistent walk with God.

4. Believe God according to the miracles. Numbers 14:22-24 says, *"Because all those men which have seen my glory, and my miracles, which I did in Egypt and in the wilderness, and have tempted me now these ten times, and have not hearkened to my voice; Surely they shall not see the land which I sware unto their fathers, neither shall any of them that provoked me see it: But my servant Caleb, because he had another spirit with him, and hath followed me fully, him will I bring into the land whereinto he went; and his seed shall possess it."* God has shown Himself to my husband and me in some amazing ways. As a pastor's wife, I do not look at the "giant" fears which loom before me. Instead, I base my faith on the "giant" miracles that God has already performed.

I want whatever God wants for my life. More importantly, I want all that God wants for my husband and for my children. I do not want to make God angry by discouraging God's people, especially the ones who are dearest on earth to me—my family. Because of this, I will not rebel against God's will for my life, I will love and not fear the people who are a part of God's will for me, I will bask in the glory that God is with me, and I will believe God according to His miracles...and what about the giants? What giants? I don't see any giants at all!

*Living on
the Bright Side
As a P.K.!*

Danger! Rough Road Ahead!

When my husband and I were dating, we had the privilege of eating lunch with another preacher's kid. He was the son of a well-known preacher, and he was much older and wiser than I. I knew there were a lot of things I could learn from him. During our meal, he mentioned the fact that preachers' kids are notoriously suspicious. I immediately identified with what he was saying; I had noticed that tendency in my own life. However, suspicion is a trap the Devil can use in the life of the preacher's kid.

Suspicion Is a Trap!

Most preachers' kids at some time in their lives will see their parents used, betrayed, and criticized. It may be that some of us will see our parents hurt by the very people they considered their friends.

If this happens, it can really be a growing time for the pastor's children. In fact, some of the sweetest teenagers I have ever met are preachers' kids who have been through church splits with their parents. However, even the best young people can find themselves becoming suspicious after they have been through something like this with their parents. If a preacher's kid is not careful, he can become one of the most skeptical and critical people around. He can become so mistrusting that he can't get help from anyone.

One of the most amazing qualities to me about my dad was his ability to trust people. Because he had worked with such a large congregation for over 40 years, he had been "burned" time and time again. However, he was not less hesitant to trust people, nor was he less able to think good of people. His attitude has helped me in many ways.

I think if parents in the ministry want to help their children overcome the pitfall of suspicion, they must display trusting attitudes in their own lives. I saw this over and over again in the lives of my parents. I also think that children need to be taught from an early age that *"love thinketh no evil."* I quote I Corinthians 13:5 often in order to help myself overcome the stumbling block of suspicion. In my own struggle with suspicion, I have learned that if you let yourself become the type of person who believes the worst about people, you will become the type of person who believes anything. If you get that way, it will be very difficult to learn the qualities of friendship and loyalty that make life so much richer.

If I suspicion something evil about someone or if I suspicion that someone is trying to take advantage of me or someone I love, I immediately take that problem to the Lord. I ask the Lord to make the truth obvious to me or to the person who could be hurt. Then, I forget about it. I do not believe evil about a person because of hearsay.

On the flip side of the coin, a preacher's kid has a lot of people in his life who love him dearly just because he is the preacher's kid. I have enjoyed growing up in the same church with the same people for almost 43 years. I have met people of all ages who have taught me the meaning of friendship and loyalty. They have shown me by example how much these qualities can enrich lives.

The older I get, the more I focus on the people who love me. This is one of the great secrets of avoiding the pitfall of suspicion. People who love me have hurt me before and may do so again, but fellowship with God's people is a great gift from the Lord, and I praise Him for it.

Avoid the Pitfall of Criticism

Next, the preacher's kid must learn to avoid the pitfall of criticism. My parents did me two great favors when I was growing up that helped me avoid this problem.

First of all, they rarely said anything bad about anybody. When I was about 15, I remember noticing that I had never heard my dad say anything bad about anyone. The same statement can be said of my mother.

Secondly, they didn't bring the problems of the ministry home. They protected us from the trials of the ministry as much as possible.

Parents do their children a great disservice when they feel free to let their criticism be spoken and their bitterness be known in the home. If I had been brought up to be a bitter and critical person, I could not possibly have survived the trials of my parents' ministry. "Love your enemies" was lived in our home; it has been my sanity during the last few years. If there is anything I desire to teach my children, it is to love their enemies. It will get them through anything. As children of a preacher, they need not only to hear this truth but also to see it in action. I praise the Lord for the privilege of seeing it myself.

Guard Against the Pitfall of Spiritual Pride

Something else we must guard against is the pitfall of spiritual pride. When I was young, there were times in my life when I was treated as if I were better than somebody else because I was the preacher's kid. My parents, however, did a lot to show me that I was no better than anyone else.

First of all, they kept me on a consistent schedule so that, believe it or not, I led a rather simple life. Our home was very organized, and our lifestyle was very simple. Our home was not at all like Grand Central Station, and considering the size of our church, that is rather amazing!

Secondly, they did not encourage talent or try to put me up in front of people a lot. They didn't pull strings to be sure I was chosen for particular groups or activities.

My parents did, however, give me a lot of praise, and they displayed a lot of confidence in my abilities. Usually, this was done privately. Therefore, it gave me a great sense of self-worth without causing me to have a superior attitude.

I was always made to feel that, in order to be a good Christian, I needed to serve the Lord like everybody else. I was made to realize that I couldn't ride along on my father's coat-tails.

I am so grateful that I was not reared to consider myself better than others. I could not have made it through the last few years if that had been my attitude. The fact that my sense of self-worth has come first from the Lord and then from my most meaningful close relationships instead of from an audience has been my mainstay.

Avoid the Pitfall of Busyness

Last of all, we must avoid the pitfall of busyness. The criticism about my dad that is the most difficult for me to bear is that he didn't spend time with us when we were children. First of all, how could anyone who didn't grow up in our home possibly know?

Of course, there were times when our dad wasn't around when we wished he could have been, but I remember my dad as never being too busy for his children. When my dad got home from church, he would stay up for hours talking to his family regardless of how late it was. He never seemed tired or burdened, and of course, his children never knew that he was.

...As a P.K.

~ 119 ~

I don't know of any of my friends whose dads stayed up until midnight talking with them around the kitchen table. My dad never seemed too busy for me; he was a lot of fun and always seemed to be happy.

My mom was always there for us, too. As I mentioned earlier, she kept us on a very strict and simple schedule. In order to keep us on that schedule, she often excused herself from activities early so that she could be at home when we got in from school. We were a priority in her life, and she was there for us.

Now my husband and I are very busy in the ministry, and we are challenged to avoid the pitfall of being too busy for our very important children. I praise the Lord for the example set by his parents and mine.

Being a Preacher's Kid Is a Rich Life!

These are the four things that stand out in my mind as possible pitfalls for the preacher's kid. With the Lord's help, these things have actually been turned into assets for me in many ways. Being a preacher's kid is a rich life—a perfect mixture of the bitter and the sweet. I wouldn't trade my life for anyone else's. I praise the Lord for my parents and the special calling God gave them.

The Importance of Meekness

"*I therefore, the prisoner of the Lord, beseech you that ye walk worthy of the vocation wherewith ye are called, With all lowliness and meekness, with longsuffering, forbearing one another in love; Endeavoring to keep the unity of the Spirit in the bond of peace.*" (Ephesians 4:1-3)

Do you feel unworthy as you begin to teach your Sunday school class, lead a soul to Christ, etc.? I often feel unworthy to stand before a group of college girls and tell them how to be a good wife. And I believe, if the truth were known, most preachers' kids (especially pastors' children) feel unworthy to be in a preacher's family. They feel unworthy as they are being watched and as great expectations are being placed upon them even at a very young age.

I know that we can never be worthy of being used of God. I could never be worthy of being the daughter of Dr. and Mrs. Jack Hyles. But the Bible tells us in Ephesians 4:1 that we can walk worthy of wherever God calls us and of whatever He calls us to do. Though this article can be applied to preachers' wives and to anyone who serves the Lord, I want to especially apply it to preachers' kids and to those who rear them.

Ephesians 4:2 tells us that the first virtues necessary in order to walk worthy of our calling are lowliness and meekness. I looked up these words in a Bible dictionary and discovered these meanings.

1. Meekness starts with an inward spirit toward God in accepting His dealings as good. In order for preachers' kids to walk worthy of their calling, they must accept their lot in life. I often hear preachers' kids make such statements as these:

- "Why did I have to be born into this family?"
- "Why do people always have to be watching me?"
- "Why do I always have to sit at the head table at banquets?"
- "Why is so much expected of me?"
- "Why do I have to set the standard and be different?"
- "Why do my parents have to be so busy in the church?"

I must admit that being watched is difficult, especially when you're just a child and you do not feel any different from anyone else. But each time a preacher's kid complains about his lot in life, he is revealing that he has not even begun to develop the virtue of meekness in his life, and he is not learning to walk worthy of his calling.

God places each of us where He does for an important purpose. I don't know why He puts us where He does, but I trust Him to put us where it is best. As a parent of preacher's kids, I can do them a great favor by being an example of contentment over my lot in life.

2. Meekness means accepting the injuries of others. Wherever there are people, there are injuries inflicted from one person to another. This is not unique to a preacher's kid. However, there are certain injuries that are typical for a preacher's kid to face. I am fortunate in that most of the people at First Baptist Church have showered their love upon me as their preacher's kid. However, I have heard such statements as this in my lifetime, sometimes toward me and sometimes toward preachers' kids with whom I have counseled:

- "You just got that position because you are a preacher's kid."
- "I don't care who you think you are, everyone is going to behave in this class."

- "He is just dating you because of who you are."
- "The preacher's kids are usually the worst kids in the church."

Preachers' kids oftentimes have to endure the injury of a church split and of watching their parents hurt by others. However, some of the greatest Christians I have met across the country are preachers' kids who have endured the pain of a church split with their parents. Perhaps, it is because they have had to learn the virtue of meekness and lowliness. A verse that I have quoted under my breath many times when feeling I was being viewed in a critical way as a preacher's kid is Philippians 2:7 and 8, which says, *"But made himself of no reputation, and took upon him the form of a servant, and was made in the likeness of men: And being found in fashion as a man, he humbled himself, and became obedient unto death, even the death of the cross."*

3. **Meekness means the opposite of self-assertiveness.** A truly meek preacher's kid will avoid statements like the following:

- "I wish my parents would spend more time with me."
- "I should have been chosen for that. They overlooked me because I'm the preacher's kid."

4. **Meekness means not thinking of one's self at all.** The best thing parents can do for their preacher's kids is to get them involved in the ministry themselves. Our daughter Jaclynn has been involved in bus work since she was eight years old. Though I do not claim that she is perfect or that she has a perfect mother, I believe that she has developed a unique compassion for others through this ministry. Children involved in a ministry are more likely to understand the importance of their parents' callings. They are more likely to be grateful for the parents God has given them. They are less likely to be concerned with things like designer clothes and their own reputations.

I remember as a child and as a teenager feeling awkward

about being introduced as a preacher's daughter. Words like, "I have always wanted to meet you," or "I have always wondered what Brother Hyles' children were like," often made me wish I was taller or more poised. I learned as an older teenager to forget about myself and to make eye contact with the person I was meeting. My new goal in meeting them became that of making them feel better about themselves after they had left me. I did not realize that I was learning the first virtue necessary for a preacher's kid. I was learning the virtue of lowliness and meekness. Of course, I still have much to learn.

Yet, how wonderful God is to give us a method for walking worthy of His calling upon our lives. Truly, I could never possibly be worthy of the wonderful Christian parents I had in Dr. and Mrs. Jack Hyles. Yet God shows me that the virtues needed to walk worthy of my calling are available to everyone. Anyone can be humble!

"Lord, help me to walk worthy of Your calling—in lowliness and meekness."

Teaching Meekness to Preachers' Kids

In the previous chapter, I shared with you the first virtues necessary for a preacher's kid to walk worthy of his calling. The following are some ideas to help a parent to train his children along this line.

1. **Be content with your own lot in life.** Let the children hear you talk often about how wonderful it is to be a preacher's wife. Brag on all the things that God has given you and don't complain about them. For example, say things like, "Isn't our house beautiful!" instead of, "I wish we could have something bigger!"

2. **Plan excitement when your husband is particularly busy.** When you find yourself very busy, take a mini-break to do something fun with your children.

3. **Allow your children to talk with you about the injuries of others and about the pressures they feel.** I realize that the line must be drawn somewhere or this will become a gossip session, but I do believe that communication is especially important in the parent/child relationship. I always felt like I could talk to my parents about everything. They may have had to correct what I said, but they finished listening first and then corrected gently.

4. **Recognize that your children are under pressure and let them hear you say so.** Statements such as, "You're just ungrateful. You could have been born in a drunkard's home, you know," are not helpful. I believe that children who have

understanding parents are less likely to complain and gossip than those who don't.

5. Respond to your children's hurts with understanding, but don't respond with anger toward the person or thing that has hurt them. Gently try to make them understand the feelings and hurts of others when they are hurt themselves. But listen first and always respond gently.

6. Do not be overly competitive and become angry when your child is not chosen for a particular task. I think a parent should hurt with the child when he is not chosen, but the parent should not become angry.

7. Get your children involved in a ministry and be involved yourself. Ask your children to get involved with you as you help others. For example, take your child with you to purchase clothes for bus kids or to make care packages for missionaries.

8. Help your child plan ways to honor their leaders, grandparents, and so forth. I have taught my children to honor their grandparents because of their position in their lives. I have never made a big deal about their grandparents' reputation or fame.

9. Help your child plan ways to honor their friends at school. Choose friends with whom they may sometimes clash or friends who may be less popular. Help your child plan birthday surprises for some of the less popular students.

10. Pray for and don't look down upon less spiritual students at school. I wouldn't want my children to make these children their best friends, but they are not to treat them as outcasts.

11. Praise your children a lot. I have always been aware that my children might have to be mellowed a bit so that God can use them. They have a lot going for them and receive much attention just because of whom their grandparents are. I pray often that God will mold them and make them what He wishes them to be. But I have not appointed myself chief "mellower." That is God's job, and I am sure that there will be enough hurts and failures in their lives to balance out the positive. I believe one of my main roles as a parent is to build my children's self-esteem. Most pride comes from too little self-esteem rather than too much.

Longsuffering and Forbearance/ Unity and Peace

"*I therefore, the prisoner of the Lord, beseech you that ye walk worthy of the vocation wherewith ye are called, With all lowliness and meekness, with longsuffering, forbearing one another in love; Endeavoring to keep the unity of the Spirit in the bond of peace.*" (Ephesians 4:1-3)

The following are virtues found in Ephesians 4:1-3 which can help preachers' kids to walk worthy of their calling:
1. Lowliness and meekness
2. Longsuffering and forbearance
3. Unity and peace

Lowliness and meekness are the foundational virtues necessary to possess the others. I looked up the words *longsuffering* and *forbearance* in my Bible dictionary and found them to mean the following: *to endure, to bear up under, to refrain from doing something,* or *to refrain from wrath.*

A preacher's kid who has meekness, that is, he has an inward spirit toward God in accepting His dealings as good as well as being accepting toward the injuries of others, has a good start toward displaying forbearance and longsuffering. He is ready to endure the pressure of being watched. He is able to bear up under the strain of criticism and even church splits. He does not make such statements as:
- "I can't wait to get out from under my parents' rules."
- "As soon as I'm grown, I am getting out of this place."

* "I wish I could change my name."

Instead, he is able to be kind and to love those who hurt him. He is able to be there for his parents and to actually be an encouragement to them through their toughest times, even though he may be hurting.

The final virtues necessary to walk worthy as a preacher's kid are those of unity and peace. The Bible definitions I found are as follows: *to muzzle, to be silent or still, to reconcile, friendliness, to be at peace or to bring peace to a certain situation.*

The preachers' kids should shut up! That is, they should keep their mouths shut when tempted to complain or criticize—especially about their lot in life. They should be friendly to others, especially to those who are less fortunate or popular than they are. They are able to bring peace and reconciliation to relationships where they have been injured.

But my favorite definition of these words *unity* and *peace* is *to bring peace to a certain situation.* Allow me to illustrate with the following story.

When Jaclynn was 13, I was busy getting ready to speak at our monthly meeting of the Women's Missionary Society. I was to speak around noon, and I had some chores to do before I left. I got groceries first, and then I proceeded home to put them away. After the groceries were put away and the house was in order, I had one more task to do before I could freshen up and leave for WMS. I needed to fold and put away one load of laundry.

Needless to say, I was feeling just a little bit frantic when I headed toward my clothes dryer to fold my laundry. Time was slipping away, and I wanted to be there in plenty of time to speak. I rushed to the laundry room to finish my last load of laundry. However, when I opened the dryer to pull out my load of clothes, the dryer was empty. When I looked down at my feet, I saw a laundry basket I had not noticed in my haste. It was filled with some very neatly folded clothes, and I found the following note:

My daughter had not only folded my laundry for me, but her kind note brought peace to my frenzied mind. I stood and stared misty-eyed at the laundry for a few seconds and thought the kind thoughts that mothers love to think about their daughters. The rest of the morning was just a little more peaceful. So many times Jaclynn has brought peace to her mother, who tends to be just a little bit too frenzied, with a kiss on the cheek, an "I love you," or "You're the best mom in the world."

I hesitate to brag on my own daughter. She and I still have so much to learn. Jaclynn could never be worthy of the wonderful grandparents God has given her. She does not deserve the great father she has. But she certainly is learning to walk worthy of them, and I so often get to reap the benefits.

Why can't we, as preachers' kids, learn to bring unity and peace to our situations? Why must we complain about the busy schedule of our parents? Just because at times they may seem too busy for us does not mean that we must be too busy for them. We can fill their lives with peace through simple surprises and expressions of love. That will bring us more joy than receiving would anyway.

My parents definitely took time for me when I was a child. They have been my dear friends as I have grown older. But I realize that I shared them with something that they loved as much as their own lives. I shared them with the ministry to which God had called them and to which they had given their lives. Did I feel sorry for myself? Not at all! I missed them occasionally when they were unavailable, but I am overwhelmed sometimes by the many blessings their sacrifices have provided for me and my family.

Again, I could never be worthy of the blessings I have received, but I can walk worthy.

Lord, help me to walk in unity and in peace. Help me to bring peace to the situations I encounter and thank You very, very, very, very, very much for making me a preacher's kid. Amen.

What I Have Learned About Crosses

$\mathcal{F}or$ much of my life, I winced when I heard sermons about how God cannot use a person unless he had first had tragedy in his life. I pondered my relatively secure and blessed life as a preacher's kid and supposed that God did not want to use me. I wanted so to win a crown for Jesus, but I wasn't sure if I had a cross with which to earn that crown. In the past few years, I have learned much about crosses, things that I wish I had known much sooner. I share what I have learned not in order to evoke understanding about my own crosses, but so that others might learn earlier what it took me a while to understand.

1. **I think sometimes the most difficult lesson to learn about crosses is how to recognize them.** It is sometimes easier to recognize the crosses which come into others' lives than it is to recognize our own crosses. Handicaps, illnesses, and tragedies are crosses easily recognizable. We see them in others' lives and praise the Lord that they are not our own. Yet sometimes the most outwardly blessed people (such as preachers' kids) struggle the most in their Christian lives. Why? I believe it is, in part, because they have failed to recognize their own crosses and, therefore, are not coping very well with them.

For example, a young preacher's kid came to me one day and said, "I don't know how you stand to attend your parents' church and to stay involved in their ministry, especially when there are battles. I couldn't do it because I hate pressure." I didn't respond inappropriately, but I wanted to sarcastically say,

"Well, I absolutely love pressure."

No, the truth is that I don't care for pressure. I weary of criticism and of bearing the responsibility of being a good testimony. As a child, I grew tired of feeling different—set apart. But one day the Holy Spirit gently showed me that part of the cross I was to bear was the cross of pressure. People often share with Brother Schaap and me that they question whether they are in God's will because they feel such pressure in their place of service. It was a wonderful day in my life when I recognized that pressure is a cross, and that pressure should never be a deciding factor in whether I go or stay where the Lord has led me.

Pressure in the ministry often comes in the form of people problems. I did not realize that many of my crosses would come in the form of even good people misunderstanding my parents and myself. It is much easier to recognize a cross when it comes in the form of the loss of a loved one than it is to recognize a cross of a people problem. Perhaps this is why sometimes the same person who lives triumphantly through great sorrow or loss, collapses shortly thereafter under the smaller load of a people problem. Unless you recognize your cross, you cannot deal with it as Christ would have you to do.

2. The second lesson I learned about crosses is that crosses can sometimes be confused with our own weaknesses. My husband has helped me with this in a gentle and, yet, very direct way. As a preacher's kid, it is easy to complain about the "cross" or problem of being watched by others. It is also easy to complain about having to share your parents with many other people. Many of the "crosses" we complain about are really fictitious "crosses" created by our own weaknesses.

Though I do believe God called me to a cross of sacrificing some time with my family as I share them with others, I also realize that some of my struggle with this cross has been due, in part, to my own selfishness. Many a preacher's kid needs to honestly ask herself if she is indeed struggling because of the cross of pressure or if she is really struggling with the weakness of her own rebellion.

This is a fact which must be faced in every area of life. For example, many a husband would say that his nagging wife is a "cross" which he must bear. However, the real problem may be, the fact, that he bears instead the weakness or should I say sin of not listening to or understanding his wife.

Many a wife "bears the cross" of a hot-tempered husband, while failing to realize that the real problem is her unloving and provocative words. In any area of people problems or pressure, we must ask ourselves this question: "Is this a cross which God has called upon me to bear, or is this a sin which I must confess?"

Once we have learned to recognize and differentiate between our "crosses" and our own shortcomings, we can confess and repent. Once we have done that, we can learn to bear our true crosses as Christ bore His own.

3. The third lesson I learned about crosses is to bear my crosses as Christ bore His. Allow me to share with you some observations about Christ's handling of His cross.

A. *Christ faced the cross.* He did not run away from it or try to avoid it. Every preacher's kid needs to face the fact that there are certain crosses which she is called upon to bear. She should not run from it, but rather she should accept her lot in life. She should be grateful that her small cross is not as heavy to carry as many other crosses. Every person who successfully bears a cross of pressure, a cross of people problems, or a larger cross of illness or tragedy must first face it.

B. *Christ carried His cross.* Not only did Christ not run away from His cross, but He made it His main purpose for living. It was a turning point in my teenage life as a preacher's kid when I decided to make it my purpose to honor my parents and to glorify Christ. Where once I felt pressure and rebellion, I now felt a sense of a special purpose.

C. *Christ gloried in His cross.* I believe that if we inter-viewed Jesus and asked Him what is His fondest memory of His earthly life, He would definitely tell us it was the cross. I don't believe He would refer to the many miracles He performed or to the time He was heralded as King throughout the streets of Jerusalem. His glory was His cross.

All preachers' kids should glory in the opportunity they have to be a testimony to what the preacher preaches. The most beautiful lady is the lady who glorifies in her "cross" of submission. The most pleasant children are the children who glory in their "cross" of obedience.

My prayer is that because of these truths, many readers will face their crosses in whatever form they have arrived and will not run away from them, but rather they will carry them and will glory in them.

D. *Christ looked ahead to what would come after.* Jesus bore His cross with dignity and did not run because He knew He would soon be reunited with the Father in Heaven.

I hope you will forgive my analogy, but when I think of glo-rying in the cross, I cannot help but think of the miracle of childbirth. Giving birth to a child is, perhaps, the most painful cross a mother must bear, but if you've ever been around a group of mothers, you realize that they love to talk about the travail of their labors. Why? Because the precious children have now safely arrived, and the mother now glories in her cross.

I have learned to glory in my life and in the unique crosses which God has asked me bear. Though I do not enjoy sorrow, it is the sorrowful moments on which I reflect the most fondly. And while I do not look forward to heavy crosses yet to come, my desire is to carry them and not to run from them. Why? Because I have eternity to glory in what Christ was able to do with my crosses, and I have at least a couple of hundred millions of years to have my parents all to myself.

> *In the cross, in the cross be my glory ever.*
> *Till my raptured soul shall find rest beyond the river.*

"And being found in fashion as a man, he humbled himself, and became obedient unto death, even the death of the cross. Wherefore God also hath highly exalted him, and given him a name which is above every name." (Philippians 2:8-9)

Balance:

The Busyness of Life

Allow me to introduce myself. I am the wife of a busy preacher. I am the mother of a ten-year-old boy. At this writing, I am the mother of a teenager—a 14-year-old girl. I am the "mother" (?) of a six-year-old toy terrier dog (whom I love, but my husband does not). I am also the "wicked stepmother" (?) of a six-week-old golden lab (whom my husband loves, but whom I do not all of the time).

May I share with you about my morning routine…some of the time anyway? I usually try to settle down some time between 5:00 and 5:30 in the morning for Bible reading and prayer. However, about the time I take my first sip of coffee and begin having my devotions in the quiet of the morning—which happens to be my favorite time of the day, my husband's dog begins to bark.

Because we are in the midst of "potty training," I immediately excuse myself from my devotions and run to the aid of my husband's dog. As soon as I am assured that my carpet will remain clean and safe from my husband's dog (whom my husband promises will be moved out of the house and into his coop in the garage in *just* 16 days), I settle down to read again.

My jealous silky terrier sees that Dusty (my husband's dog) has received my attention, so Shadow (my wonderful dog) jumps in my lap and sits on top of the Bible. I think of explaining about the preserved King James Bible and how he ought to respect it, but instead, I move him a few inches and pet him for a few minutes. I then place Shadow on the floor and begin again to read God's Word.

Unexpected Interruptions Will Happen

My husband then jumps out of the shower and sticks his head out the door. "Cindy," he says, "I have an early appointment this morning, so I need breakfast ready an hour earlier…in ten minutes from now!"

I want to say, "But I'm reading my Bible!" Somehow it doesn't sound right, so I go to fix breakfast instead.

When everyone is fed, I put the breakfast dishes on hold, and again, I settle into my favorite place with my favorite Book for my favorite time.

Then Jaclynn calls, "Mom, I need my cheerleading uniform, and we just had a game yesterday. Is it clean?"

I reply, "It's in the washing machine and soaking wet. I didn't know you needed it again today. I will put it in the dryer for you."

It isn't long until Kenny yells and wants to know if his plaid shirt looks all right with his striped tie and where his other cleat is. He must have it for his game this evening.

Perhaps you can relate to this description of some of my mornings. You intend to walk closely with the Lord; but the busyness of life with a family presses in on you, and problems begin before you even have time to gather enough sweet spirit from God's Word to help you through the day. Perhaps, like myself, your days sometimes consist of little league games and events which make you madder at the umpire instead of closer to the Lord. Your life is spent in the car, and though you intend to get some praying in at the red lights, you spend your time instead refereeing arguments or answering hard questions about dating and teenage life.

You change your devotional time to afternoon and emergencies arise. So you change it to the evening and fall asleep before you've finished verse one.

Though my devotional life is quite consistent, and I am really only describing an occasional morning, I do have mornings mentioned like those above. I have mornings where my heart feels cold toward the Lord.

I know I am giving my best to do what I think God wants me to be doing at any given moment...yet my heart grows weary...and cold. And I mistakenly believe that God's love for me must have grown cold also. Then I am reminded on a Sunday morning by my pastor/father of the verses in Romans 8:38, 39 which say, *"For I am persuaded, that neither death, nor life, nor angels, nor principalities, nor powers, nor things present, nor things to come, Nor height, nor depth, nor any other creature, shall be able to separate us from the love of God, which is in Christ Jesus our Lord."*

The Lord draws my attention to the word *"life."* I have always felt I understood what God was saying when He assured me that death would not separate me from Him. What a comfort to know He will go through death with me and meet me in Heaven. I thought I understood what God was saying when He says that "powers" can't separate His love from me. The Devil himself can't take away God's love, nor can any enemy I might encounter.

But what I needed on that Sunday morning was to know that the busyness of life couldn't separate God's love from me...not new puppies or early breakfasts or laundry or missing socks. No, not even sports games or taxi-cab driving or constant interruptions can separate me from God's love. Though I may feel that I have failed in my time with God and though I may feel too pulled apart by responsibilities, nothing can separate me from the love of God.

I write this chapter to encourage busy mothers with some words which greatly encouraged me one Sunday morning years ago. For I've noticed in my own life that when my heart is breaking through trials, God's love just naturally seems close by. But when my heart is cold and hardened because of a too-busy schedule, I fool myself by thinking that God's heart is cold and hardened also. When I believe this to be true, I am hardened further, and I lose my desire to walk closely to the Lord.

When I realize that God's love is just as near when I have failed Him in my busyness, I become more determined to make the necessary reorganizations to try again to spend my time with Him. How wonderful to know that the busyness of life cannot separate me from the love of God...not being a wife, not being a mother of a sports-enthused boy or of a teenage girl, or not being the owner of a wonderful terrier (my dog) or of a wonderful new puppy (my husband's dog to which I'm becoming awfully attached!) Nothing can separate me from the love of God—not even the busyness of my life.

Dear Lord, it is for Your unfailing love that we praise Thee. And I love You, too, my Friend...very, very much!

Loving People When You Are Busy

Even while growing up in the home of a man who well could have been the busiest man in the world, I always felt loved. I am now married to a man who is a child of two extremely successful business people, and yet, he often recounts to me his memories of love and complete security. My husband and I strive with bull-dog determination to make our children feel loved in spite of increasingly busy schedules. That is what I believe it takes to make people feel loved when you are busy—bulldog determination. I cannot share with you ideas which will guarantee successful child rearing. I wish that I could.

I have no guarantees to offer you; however, I can tell you some principles and ideas that my husband and I have set for our family. Most of them were adopted from our own parents, and I can guarantee their effectiveness in making children feel loved—for we, as children, truly did feel especially loved.

• **Have principles about being away from the family and stick to them.** This is especially important for a mother. For instance, when I had small children, I traveled just a little bit to women's meetings. Though I loved everything that I did, including traveling, when I say "a little bit," I mean a little bit. My husband and I discussed together how many out-of-town engagements I would take, and I did not exceed that number. I also required a certain amount of advance notice before I traveled. I did not leave town as a way to help someone who had a last minute cancellation and was in a bind. I would have loved to help in those kinds of situations, but while I had small children, it was my belief that I could not. I did not like to "spring" leaving town suddenly upon my family.

• **Let your family know you are available whenever they need you.** When my son Kenny complained one evening that I had to go to the church to speak at a ladies' meeting, I suggested that he go with me, and he did. Though I am home most evenings throughout the year, I reminded my children that there was never a time that they could not go with me to a meeting if they wished to go. When you leave to go somewhere, inform your children of exactly where you are going, how long you will be gone, and where they can reach you if they need you. Make them feel that you could be interrupted no matter what you are doing. My parents practiced this with me, and to be honest, it made me feel less likely to interrupt, not more likely. Yet, it made me feel loved and secure.

• **As much as possible, include your children in everything you do.** When my husband's parents started a business, they did much of the work themselves with their 12-year-old son by their side. That 12-year-old son became my husband. Working side by side with his parents all of his teenage years not only taught him hard work, but it also taught him how to love and be loved. My own children and I did most of our work together, especially in the summertime. I never enjoyed leaving my children with baby sitters unless it was absolutely necessary, and therefore, it seems that we have been everywhere and done everything together. I did, and still do, however, consider my weekly date with my husband absolutely necessary. It is the one part of my life in which my children were left out, and they knew that mom and dad needed to be alone.

• **Work side by side with your children.** My dad advised me when my children were younger to make teaching them to work a top priority. He said that teaching a child to work is more important for a mother than to teach them the Bible. The father can be the primary Bible teacher in the family. It is honestly a sacrifice in the beginning to teach children to work, but in the end it reaps tremendous benefits and precious memories for everyone.

• **Keep your personal work as separate as possible from your family.** I have no problem with women working separate jobs in the home. It is often a good alternative for extra income. However, I think that every worker should separate her work from her family as much as possible. I must admit that I was not the first to pick up my children from school. They played for a half-hour every day after school. But when I picked up my children from school, nine times out of ten, I had put in a hard day's work, and I was ready to completely devote my time to helping with homework, teaching, playing, etc., with my family. Through the years, I also tried to protect my children from the burdens of our ministry. They knew very little of the burdens that our church was facing. We reserved their right to enjoy their childhood and did not "bog" them down with our problems. My parents afforded us the privilege to enjoy our childhood, and I appreciate it greatly.

• **Be sure that you do not put your children in bed at night without having enjoyed some quality time with them.** I had a scheduled time to play with my children every evening that we were home. If I had more children, I perhaps would have spent time with a different child each night once weekly. Of course, there were occasions when our time together was not possible. When these times occurred, I spent at least some time with my children anyway, whether it was just giving a five-minute back rub or something simple, I strove to always have daily quality time with them. My dad helped me one day by giving me this advice: Keep your children up one hour later, if needs be, so that they can have quality time with their parents.

- **Make "getting up" and "going to bed" time especially enjoyable.**
- **Make riding in the car time enjoyable.**
- **Eat as many meals together as possible.**
- **Have family slogans and family songs.** Our family slogan was "Us Four and No More"! This slogan was adopted from my husband's family. I have family songs that I wrote for my children. Through the years, I sang the same lullaby to my children each night. It was one that I wrote for them. Friends would spend the night and ask me to write down the words for their parents.

I heard our high school principal, Dr. Don Boyd, say something like this: "Children who obey because they love and feel loved will obey forever, because love is forever. Children who obey because of fear will obey until they are away from their parents."

I truly felt loved as a child and still want to obey and honor because of that love. I wish, with bulldog determination, to love my children even while my husband and I busily and happily serve the One Who first loved us.

When a Schedule Is Too Busy

In this chapter, allow me to give you some ideas on how to control a busy schedule. These ideas, in turn, will help you get your children scheduled.

1. Take your phone off the hook for a few hours each day. Too many of us think the phone has to control us. Schedule some work hours for each day in which you will not answer the phone. When you are spending time with your family, have your children answer the phone and take a message.

2. Keep the television off. If you have difficulty controlling it, get rid of it or put it in an out-of-the-way place. Most (95%) of the time, television should not be on at all. Learn what motivates you to work hard. For example, melancholy music, even if it is spiritual, does not motivate me to hard work. Sermon tapes or praise music motivates me when I am doing those "mindless" tasks of housekeeping.

3. Spend evening hours with your family. The reason I schedule only certain hours to work and place importance on finishing that work is so that I can be available to my family during the evening hours. I have striven, as my children have been growing, to have a fun time with them in the evening. I highly recommend it. The fun time should be early in the evening before mother starts wilting!

My husband and I have a scheduled date on Friday evenings. I have a lighter schedule on Fridays so that I might not be that "wet dishrag" on Friday evenings.

4. Have a ministry day. It is hard for a mother to commit herself to a soul-winning ministry. Most mothers join a ministry slowly and quit quickly. If they do go soul winning, they can't wait until their hour is up so they can go home to finish their work. It has been a help to me to schedule my time so that my weekly work is accomplished by Saturday (my ministry day). That way I can visit my Sunday school class, my husband's bus route or go soul winning and not be distracted by other duties. The Devil still tries to distract me with small things here and there, but it is easier for me to be effective if I have a day set aside just for ministry. (I visit with my family at least part of the time on Saturday, which also gives me precious time with them.)

5. **Schedule some time for yourself each day.** For example, when my children were young, I took a nap each day. I feel less need for one now; but when my body starts to become weary, I will take one once in a while. I love to read, and I spend 30 minutes to an hour reading each day. This is my special time for myself. Also, allow yourself some time to freshen up once or twice a day. If you have been too busy to freshen up and to make a big deal when your husband arrives home, you have been too busy.

6. **Reorganize frequently.** If the truth were known, most of us tend toward disorganization. We need frequent times of reorganization just like we need a bath every day. Write out a new schedule, perhaps every fall when the kids go back to school, every New Year's Day (Who doesn't need to reorganize after Christmas?), and at the beginning of every summer. Write down your new schedule. Create a loose schedule and follow it strictly!

7. **Reorganize your things frequently.** Go through your closets, drawers, etc., once every three or four months. I have read many books on the subject of organization and have found these three suggestions most helpful:

a. *Get rid of the things you don't need.*

b. *Use containers or dividers.* For example, a sock drawer can be divided by using pretty baskets, plastic organizers or just shoe boxes. No matter how neatly we stack our socks on reorganization day, they will run into each other in a few weeks when we hurriedly throw them into the drawer. This is helpful, especially in organizing a drawer where many different things must be stored in one drawer.

c. *Reorganize frequently.* You will find that the more you separate, using containers, the less time it will take to reorganize.

8. Be patient with yourself. Though I believe we need to set the pattern of organization for our children, I also realize that life does not always run by our own designed schedules. It seems a wife's and mother's middle name should be "flexible." But this is not an excuse for disorganization. It is the disorganized who need a schedule the most. Therefore, we should always keep trying. In the process of trying, however, don't compare yourself with others or "rake yourself over the coals." Realize that reorganization is frequently a necessary part of life, and what works for another woman may not work for you. Be willing to learn from others and keep on trying, but be patient with yourself and with the disorganization of those you love.

Remember that all of our character is pretty poorly formed without the Holy Spirit working in us. So yield to Him and ask Him to lead you to develop habits of organization.

Thoughts on Recession

"*Mommy,*" my daughter Jaclynn asked one day, "is Susie* poor?"

"Jaclynn, what do you think it means to be rich?" I answered her question with a question. "Is a person rich because they have a lot of money or is a person rich because they have a lot of friends?"

"Oh, Mommmmmmmmm! I suppose a person is rich because they have a lot of friends."

"Jaclynn, does Susie have a lot of friends?"

"Mom, I really believe that Susie has more friends than anyone in our school."

"Well then, Jaclynn, I guess she must be rich."

(* name changed)

I find in my own life a great temptation to put improper value on material things. Looking around on the value system of the society in which I have grown up, I can understand why. Yet my parents taught me from the time I was a little child that there were many things that were more important than money. Several times as a child I heard my dad preaching on the sin of loving money. During some of these sermons, I actually saw my dad rip up a dollar bill as a way of displaying his disgust for the sin of materialism. This object lesson still convicts me as a 42-year-old adult, and I long to share its lessons with my own children. I know I make it difficult for my children to choose full-time Christian service when I overemphasize money and material things. Perhaps you share this same burden to avoid materialism in your home. If so, let me share with you some ideas about how we can strive to do so.

1. Never differentiate between the rich and the poor. Perhaps you could tell by the conversation I have included at the beginning of this article that I try to avoid labeling anyone as rich or poor in front of my children.

2. Always identify with the person who has less. Whenever I find myself in a group of people from different financial circumstances, I always try to identify with the person who has less. My desire is to make everyone feel comfortable around me; but if that is not possible, I want to make the less fortunate feel comfortable.

The Bible has much to say about he who "considers the poor." *"Blessed is he that considereth the poor: the Lord will deliver him in time of trouble."* (Psalm 41:1) When Jesus was on this earth, He chose to identify with the poor. I am sure He could have chosen to be born in the Conrad Hilton of Bethlehem. However, He chose to be born in a manger to a couple of limited financial means.

My prayer as I decorate my home, choose my fashion of dress, etc., is that I would choose that which is lovely without choosing that which is intimidating to those who might have less.

3. Never buy something new because you are depressed or unhappy. If I could think of the most common temptation women face, I think it would be this: We are tempted to find our satisfaction and/or our self-esteem in material things. When we handle our depression by buying a new dress, a new item for our home, or a new item of make-up, we are merely putting a bandage on our wound of dissatisfaction or poor self-esteem. The wound will have to constantly be re-bandaged, and it will never heal until we learn to find our complete satisfaction and self-esteem in Christ.

Because of this, I force myself *not* to buy something new when I am having a bad day, even if I can afford it. Rather, I schedule times during the year when I will make new purchases for my home, my wardrobe, etc., and I forget about these things at other times. Of course, I plan my shopping schedule around times when I know that certain items will be on sale.

Children quickly pick up the attitude that money solves all problems. However, this idea is a false perception and will only lead them into misery. On the flip side of the coin, I try not to say things to my children like, "I cannot buy you that because we don't have enough money." I do not want money to be a topic of discussion in our home, either negatively or positively.

4. Remember where others are and where you used to be. My husband is a bus captain in East Chicago, Indiana. Each Saturday he and our daughter Jaclynn go bus calling together. On Saturdays, Jaclynn sees what the world is really like. She sees sin not as it is displayed on television advertisements and on billboards, but as it is displayed in ruined lives. She also sees much poverty. It is not unusual for Jaclynn to arrive home from bus calling only to heave a great big sigh and say, "It is so good to be home." I have seen some of the homes where Jaclynn visits, so I know what she is saying. She is saying that she is grateful for what she has. Nothing can better stop us in our struggle to get more and more than to look for a few moments at the needs on the other side of the fence.

5. Stress joy rather than attainment in your home. Our son Kenny once expressed a desire to sell our home and move into a *great big* house. I asked Kenny if he knew he would be happy in a *great big* house. He said that he was not sure. I then asked him if he felt our family was happy in the home in which we live now. He said, "Yes." I then said, "Kenny, it seems awfully silly to me to move into another house when we are already happy in this one."

I am not saying a Christian should never move into a *great big* house. I *am* saying that Brother Schaap and I have made a decision that we would not move unless the Lord kicked us out of the house in which we now live. We also made a decision to enjoy our home. Rarely a day goes by that I do not share with my husband how much I enjoy our home. I would imagine his financial pressure is eased somewhat by knowing that his wife is satisfied.

6. Memorize Bible verses that de-emphasize money. Some examples of these verses are I Timothy 6:6-10, 17; Psalm 49; Psalm 62:10; Proverbs 11:4, 23:5, 30:8-9; and Luke 12:16-34.

In conclusion, let me say that I do not share these things because I am a shining example of them, but rather because I am a young girl who has grown up in affluent America during one of its most prosperous and materialistic eras. Because of this, I constantly find ways that my attitude needs improving about material things.

Recently, I was reading a book by Corrie Ten Boom who spent several months in solitary confinement in a Nazi prison camp. In this book Corrie said that a person is rich who has the privilege of seeing another human face. I have often thought of that statement while sitting in the First Baptist Church auditorium among thousands of not just human, but also Christian, faces. According to Corrie Ten Boom's definition, I am a very rich lady.

Jaclynn told me the other day that she has seven Bibles of her own in her own bedroom. I remembered the stories I have been told about people in foreign countries who long for a few pages from the Word of God. "Jaclynn," I said, "you're rich."

Often there is talk in America about recession. Having never lived through the Great Depression, I am sure I can't fully understand its threat. Yet when I consider the values that

I have been taught since childhood and count the blessings in my own family, home, and church, I can only come to one conclusion. *There is no recession here!* May we teach our children the Christian value system that does not decline with the economy. Decide to live frugally regardless of any positive change in your financial condition. Let me share with you some ways to save money.

   I. Save money on groceries.
     A. Shop once a week and don't shop between times.
     B. Cut back on cleaning supplies. I like my house clean, but most cleaning supplies are unnecessary.
     C. Clip coupons.
     D. Shop at discount grocery stores.
     E. Watch for sales at regular grocery stores.

  II. Save money on clothing.
     A. Watch for sales at better stores. Buy your wardrobe basics and dressy clothes at these times. (For example, on Labor Day and after Christmas, many quality stores mark down clothes as much as 75%.
     B. Shop at thrift stores and less expensive stores for casual clothes and extra items.

 III. Save money on others.
     A. Take the time to make or buy a card or write a note rather than buy an expensive gift.
     B. Be on time with your gifts. I find that I spend more on a gift when it is a belated one. The thought loses much of its value after the big day is over.
     C. Don't try to have the most expensive gift.
     D. Space out phone calls and call when rates are cheaper.
     E. Learn others' tastes so that you can be thoughtful without spending a lot. Take note of collections, etc.

F. When having a Sunday school class party, ask members to bring a *small* fee. Keep it small.

IV. Save money on home decorations.
  A. Look for items that will not go out of style quickly.
  B. Look for items that will truly fit your personality rather than choosing trendy items.
  C. Look for the best quality at the best price.
  D. Shop at discount stores for less expensive items (e.g., place mats, utensils, etc.)

V. Save money on miscellaneous activities.
  A. Schedule luxury. For example, I make one relatively fancy meal a week. The rest of my home-cooked meals are very simple to cut down on grocery bills.
  B. Learn to enjoy simple restaurants and cut coupons for them.
  C. Learn to do things yourself as time and weather permits. (e.g., Do your own gardening, wash your own car, and clean your own carpet.) My children help me with many of these chores. It is fun and builds character.
  D. *Don't window shop!* Go into a store to get what you planned to buy and then leave. If you see something you need that was not on your list, write it down and purchase it the next week or with the next paycheck.
  E. Don't tour model homes! Some people tour homes and search magazines for ideas. This is a good idea if you already have money set aside for a particular project. Otherwise, don't look! If you are like me, you already have more ideas than you have money.

The Best Thing You Can Do for Your Child

$\mathcal{I}$ expressed some concerns to my dad one day about my son Kenny and his spiritual life. During our conversation, I told my dad, "Kenny is 'crazy' about his dad."

My dad assured me that Kenny's being "crazy" about his dad was more important at this point in his life than anything else. This thought sobered me because I was reminded that if Kenny was crazy about his dad, I would probably need to be the one to make it so. I realize that my husband can make himself a hero to our son without my help. However, I also realize that I most likely have the ability to knock that hero down a peg or two in Kenny's eyes.

This conversation with my dad turned my thoughts to a verse which my husband showed me some time ago. *"And he shall turn the heart of the fathers to the children, and the heart of the children to their fathers, lest I come and smite the earth with a curse."* (Malachi 4:6) I believe that the best thing I can do for my children is to turn their hearts toward their father (even if that means turning their hearts away from me).

In the household in which I grew up, my father was the most important part of our home. My mother scheduled our time so that our lives revolved around his schedule and his ministry. My mother often took a back seat and stood in the shadows as we made a hero out of our dad. As a young girl, I remember a particular moment when I think that my heart left my body and was given to my dad. On that day, a Daddy's girl was born. I did all that I could from that time on to be an encouragement to my dad and to really know my dad. I believe that my mother allowing me this privilege is perhaps the best thing she ever did for me. Marriage was not much of an adjustment for me because I was used to spoiling the head of the house.

Today, however, the average mother is turning her children's hearts away from their father. That is one reason why I do not watch modern television programs. On most of these shows, the father is made to look like an idiot. Truly in our day, the hearts of the children have been turned away from the fathers, and truly, we have been smitten with a curse. I believe that curse is homosexuality and AIDS. My husband and father have both said that they have never counseled a homosexual who did not have a domineering mother and who did not hate his father. I do not wish to condemn those who have a loved one who is homosexual and yet these two common denominators are only two of three that have been found in their counseling experiences.

> *There is only one thing which completely hinders a woman from accomplishing what a man accomplishes.*

I also believe there is another curse in our nation which is a result of our hearts being turned away from our fathers. That curse is abortion. Mothers wish to be as good as fathers. They wish to be able to run for president of the country and of the corporation just as their husbands can. There is only one thing which completely hinders a woman from accomplishing what a man accomplishes. That is the "inconvenience" of pregnancy and childbirth. I have no doubt that the "free choice" expressed by liberal and other women in this country is just their way of trying to be as good as or better than dad. I suppose just about every curse we have in America today, such as teen suicide, can point back to the breakdown to the mother's lack of willingness to make dad the king of our hearts.

We just don't seem to be able to understand that God created submission and the headship of the home to benefit everyone involved. I believe that submission is the best child rearing tool a mother has. Because of this, allow me to give you some ideas about how to turn your children's hearts toward their father.

I. Be willing to be #2. Kenny teasingly told me one day that he loved dad more than me. I said, "That's okay, because I love dad more than I love you, too." I Peter 3:4 says that ladies are to adorn themselves with a meek and quiet spirit. Being quiet does not mean that we do not speak above a whisper. Being quiet means that we do not demand our own rights; we are willing to take second place. The following are some ways to be #2.

    A. Encourage your kids to be close to their dad.

    B. Plan special activities rather than being negative and critical when dad is busy. This will prevent preachers' kids from being sour about the ministry.

    C. Respond to Dad's arrivals and departures to and from home.

    D. Wave to Dad as he drives away until he is out of sight. This is usually practiced in our home.

    E. Have kids make Dad breakfast to eat in bed.

    F. Have kids greet him at the door with his favorite snack or with his favorite newspaper. The dad of our home loves *USA Today*.

    G. Have kids give him back rubs.

    H. Have kids bring Dad his favorite drink in bed.

I. Respect his privacy and his need to rest.

J. Encourage your kids to run errands with Dad.

K. Make signs for him.

L. Change your schedule to eat meals with him.

M. Be a peacemaker. Don't come between Dad and your children. Especially when my kids were young, they would come to me for a hug after daddy had spanked them. I always told them that they would have to go hug their dad, and then they could come hug me.

II. **Be willing to follow.** Here's how:
   A. Refer your children's questions to their dad when he is home.
   B. Agree with Dad's discipline.
   C. Allow Dad to make even the small decisions in the home. A man who cannot quickly make small decisions will not be able to make good big decisions. When he places the decision on you, kindly toss it back to him with praise and confidence.
   D. Yield to him in conflict. Yield in control of the thermostat, in the matter of who gets the bathroom first, etc.
   E. Yield to him in your body language by following his lead as you walk in public and by being pleasant in your expressions toward him.

III. **Be willing to honor Dad.** Here's how:
   A. Brag on him.
   B. Call him into the room, and you and your children give him a standing ovation.
   C. Stand up for him as his defender to the children.
   D. Cover for him.
   E. Take the blame for him. This is very Christlike, as Jesus took the blame for us.

I present this information not as that which I have followed as a perfect example. I present it as something I try to follow and as something which was followed to a great degree in my childhood.

Living
on the Bright Side
As a Godly Wife

Different, but Not Inferior

A graduate student at Hyles-Anderson College asked me this question: "What are the qualifications for a wife?" She had heard my husband say in one of his classes that it is more important to be qualified to do something than it is to actually have the opportunity to do it.

I have taught many verses in the Bible which are written to wives about marriage. But I must admit that her question stumped me just a bit. The only verse which came to my mind was I Timothy 3:11 which says, *"Even so must their wives be grave, not slanderers, sober, faithful in all things."* I promised my student that I would study this verse. This verse is talking about deacons' wives. Yet surely, if God wishes deacons' wives to have these qualities, He would certainly be pleased if all wives possessed these qualities.

The quality I wish to expound upon is that quality which is described by these words, *"not slanderers."* When I met my husband, I was fascinated with the differences in our personalities. The word which came to my mind so often when describing my husband was "stable." But I found shortly after marriage, the very quality which a bride loves in her husband often shows its liability. Every personality asset does have a liability, you know.*

I discovered that stable people often seem non-reactive (especially to more unstable people like myself who are impatient and usually in a hurry). If a wife is not careful, she will develop a critical spirit toward her husband and will become a slanderer. She will look down on the very qualities which once attracted her to her husband.

Personality Differences

In this chapter, let me point out the following personality differences:

Introvert — Some spouses draw strength from being alone.

Extrovert — Some spouses draw strength from being with people.

Idealists — Some people tend to have their heads in the clouds. They enjoy philosophizing and dreaming about the future.

Realists — Some people are realistic. They rely on facts and past information to form their opinions rather than idealistic dreaming.

Logical — Some people are cut and dried in the disciplining of the children.

Emotional — Some people think with their emotions. They have a difficult time being consistent in disciplining children.

Scheduled — Some people love routine.

Nonscheduled — Some people are flexible and feel stifled by a routine.

Leaders — Some people create their own ideas.

Followers — Some people carry out the ideas of others.

People-Oriented — Some people put aside tasks to help others.

Task-Oriented — Some people follow lists and help people when their tasks are finished or at a scheduled time.

Perfectionists — Some people tend to be slower in their work, but they care for details in a perfect manner.

Performers — Some people tend to be very quick, but do not always care for details.

Obviously, it would be ideal if we were all the perfect balance of these characteristics like Jesus was. If we think we are, we probably have been fooling ourselves. I believe the most balanced people are often happily married people. Why? Because they have worked hard to learn to accept someone who is different from them in many ways. In doing so, they have freed themselves to learn from that person's strengths. It is important that we learn to accept the differences in our spouses as just that—differences. They are not inferiorities. I have never counseled an unhappily married person who did not have a superior attitude toward the differences of their spouse.

Learning to accept differences has not only helped me to deal with my husband, but also with my children. My daughter Jaclynn is a perfectionist. I am a performer. Because we have accepted each other, we work very well together. Jaclynn kindly says, "Slow down, Mom, that is not quite straight enough." I need her admonition, and I kindly say, "Jaclynn, you need to speed it up, Hon. I think you're being too picky." I don't say, "Jaclynn, why are you so slow? I think you just don't care." Nor does Jaclynn say, "Boy, Mom, you are a slob." We have discussed our differences, and we have accepted each other.

Learning to accept differences has helped me to deal with my fellow church members. All of us know someone who doesn't seem to think like we do at all in any circumstance. However, we will never learn to work well with people nor will we please the Lord when we "write off" these people as being inferior to ourselves.

My husband and I went over this list together. We laughed

as we discovered that we were exactly alike in half of the areas and exactly opposite in the other half. In one area, my husband insists that I am one way, and I insist that I am the other. We do not always think accurately about our own selves. This is another reason why we should accept the differences of others.

I suggest that you have fun with your spouse discussing these personality differences. Accept your husband and enjoy your husband as he is—different, yes, but definitely not inferior. Then you will have mastered one of the qualities of a godly wife—by not being a slanderer.

[*Used by permission from Dr. Jack Schaap]

How to Protect Your Mind

In the previous chapter, we discussed a quality that all wives ought to possess. We discussed not being a slanderer and how slander creeps into our relationships not only in our churches, but also in our families. Now I would like to focus on another quality God gives for deacons' wives, that would be wise for all wives to possess. I believe, in God's sight, it is more important to be qualified to do something than it is to actually have the opportunity to do it.

God commands deacons' wives to be sober. This word does not mean *not drunken*. Rather, it means *to be disciplined in one's thinking*. Women, especially young women, are not known for being disciplined in their thinking. We struggle with negative thoughts, such as worry, fear, criticism of self and others, jealousy and so forth. In order for a woman to be qualified as a wife, she must gain the victory over these things.

Of course, the foundational method for disciplining our minds is our daily devotional time. Getting more and more into the Bible and spending more and more time in prayer can change our thinking. The problem, however, is that it is impossible for a busy wife and mother to always be praying and reading the Bible. The key then to having disciplined thinking is to feed your mind with things during each day which would protect your mind from undisciplined thinking.

Good Ways to **Protect** Your Mind

1. Protect your mind by avoiding worldly television or videos (which are almost 100 percent of the above-mentioned.)

2.   Protect your mind by avoiding worldly music.
3.   Protect your mind by avoiding worldly radio talk shows.
4.   Protect your mind by avoiding gossip.
5.   Protect your mind by avoiding news broadcasts. I am not against listening to the news to find out what is happening. But we do not need to listen to more than a few minutes of news each day. Most of news is repetition. We really do not need to feed our minds with such news. I prefer radio news because it is less sensational than television news, and I can listen to it while my children are not home.

Good Ways to **Feed** *Your Mind*

1.   Feed your mind by singing praise music.
2.   Feed your mind by listening to sermon tapes while you are doing mundane tasks.
3.   Feed your mind by listening to positive and spiritual music.
4.   Feed your mind by keeping your mind busy, especially when you are performing tasks that do not capture your mind. Remember, an idle mind is the Devil's workshop. The idle mind will be prone to either worry or criticize (slander).
5.   Feed your mind contentment. One of the great ways for a woman to be disciplined in her thinking is for her to protect her mind from thinking about things she wishes she had and to feed her mind with thoughts about the positive qualities of the things which she does have. One of our Hyles-Anderson College teachers, Brother Larry Smith, preached a message using the verse in I Timothy 6:6 which says, *"But godliness with contentment is great gain."* He pointed out that if we are content, we can actually expect to gain. However, if we are discontent, we can expect to lose. We will lose in our relationships as well as losing materially.

Sometimes, my dad would teasingly ask me if Brother

Schaap and I were sorry we got married. We often teasingly responded that we were mutually contented. I suppose that is what is so special about being married many years. Brother Schaap and I have had time to discover our differences and to accept each other as different rather than slandering each other. Now after nearly 25 years together as husband and wife, on those days when passion is not riding as high as perhaps it should be, we can still enjoy our contentment with each other. Surely contentment has brought much gain to our relationship.

Wives need to discipline their thinking by being contented with their husbands, their children, their families, their friends, their houses, their churches and their fellow church members. Discontentment has led a lot of people out of the ministry and out of God's will. Discontentment can feel like the leading of the Holy Spirit, but it is not. We need to protect ourselves from discontentment so that we can better discern God's will for our lives. I daily ask God to protect Brother Schaap and me from discontentment as well as doing what I can do to avoid it.

Christian wives, are you contented or are you slandering the people and things around you? I do not want to know whether or not you are a wife. Rather, I would like to ask you, "According to God's measuring stick, are you qualified?"

What It Means to Be Grave

In the previous two chapters, we have discussed three qualities for wives — she is to be sober, and she is to refrain from being a slanderer. This month, I would like to discuss another quality which is "to be grave." This does not mean that a wife is to be boring or "dead" in her personality. Rather it means that she is to live a holy life which is motivated by a seriousness of hers and her husband's purpose for being on this earth.

My husband teaches foundational principles for Christian growth which can be found in Hebrews 6:1, 2 which say, *"Therefore leaving the principles of the doctrine of Christ, let us go on unto perfection; not laying again the foundation of repentance from dead works, and of faith toward God, Of the doctrine of baptisms, and of laying on of hands, and of resurrection of the dead, and of eternal judgment."* One of these is the principle of eternal judgment. That is the principle that God has a purpose for each of our lives, and we will receive eternal rewards for those things which we have done for the Lord.

Recently, after talking with a young person about her desire to make money and to succeed in a career, I wondered with great amazement how that young person could be so consumed with things that are merely temporal. Then I began to try to imagine what my goals would be like if I did not understand the principle of eternal judgment. I thought, "No wonder this young person has no seriousness of spiritual purpose. If I did not live in light of eternity, I would probably do the same."

However, somewhere along the way as a young person, I did

grasp the seriousness of my spiritual purpose. I began to see myself more in light of my eternity than in the light of my life here on this earth. I comprehended the brevity of my life, and I made it my goal to fulfill whatever purpose God had designed for my brief stay here.

You may say, "What a morbid way of thinking!" No, this way of thinking is not morbid at all. Rather, I believe those who have a seriousness of purpose enjoy life more than others. Allow me to share why:

1. Those who are grave are more contented. Though my husband provides very well for me, I accepted a long time ago that I will probably never be materially wealthy on this earth. My husband and I have both discovered that whenever we "go after money" for ourselves, God seems to close the door. Yet He seems to bless us greatly when we walk carefully in His will, not seeking wealth for ourselves, but only to use our abilities for Him.

You see, my husband is a preacher, and God has a special purpose for him. Therefore, material things can never be the main focus of our lives. Realizing and accepting this has actually freed me to be content and to enjoy life more. And it will free you also, whether you are a preacher's wife or a deacon's wife or a lay person's wife.

2. Those who are grave are not as prone to slander. Because I realize that God has a special purpose for Brother Schaap's life, I also realize that God has a special recipe of qualities which He wishes Brother Schaap to possess. I am more cautious about slandering Brother Schaap because I realize that God is at work in his life, and I do not wish to hinder the work of the Holy Spirit. Though I may at some time give Brother Schaap some constructive criticism, that criticism is rarely and prayerfully given, because I am grave about Brother Schaap's ministry and God's plan for his life.

I rarely seek to critique others because I realize, though they may be different and hard for me to understand, the reason they are different may be the different purpose God has for their lives. I realize that God has a purpose for my life as well as for theirs. There is room for all of us and there is, therefore, no need to slander others in order to exalt our own ministry.

3. Those who are grave are more prone to holiness. I believe the first time I realized the seriousness of God's purpose for my life and for my future husband was when I was a junior in high school. I did not date much my last two years of high school because I had a new vision of what God wanted to do with my life. I believe that vision kept me from dating some guys who were not what they should have been spiritually.

Throughout my life since then, I have walked guard around the walls of my purity. Why? Not because I am a great Christian, but because I do not want to miss the purpose which God has for my life.

As a wife, I must also realize that I was not primarily made for my own purposes. Rather I was made to help my husband fulfill his purpose in God's will. This is what I want in my life more than anything. I will sacrifice a few thrills, a bigger house, and the privilege of criticizing others so that God can use my husband. It's really no sacrifice at all. I do not care whether my husband was created to shine the shoes of other preachers or whether he was created to be president of the United States. I only want him to do what God made him to do. For it's then we will be content, not only temporarily, but also eternally.

May I lovingly say that if you are not serving and loving in light of the seriousness of His eternal purpose, you may be a wife, but you are not yet qualified. Why not begin to meet God's qualifications today?

Faithfulness

I have always loved to go to church. When I was a child, I must admit that church was mainly a social time. All of my friends were children in our church. As a teenager, church was a place where you went to talk to boys before and after the services. But during my teenage years, church became something else to me. I began to listen and heed the sermons which were preached, and I even began to feel a great NEED for them. I always loved to hear my pastor/father preach. I found his sermons to be profound and yet easy to be understood. They have always been what I needed. Dad often teased me as a child that I listened to preaching more than I did personal counsel, and I suppose he was right. From the time I was a teenager, I have gone into each preaching service asking myself this question, "How can this sermon change me?" In fact, every Sunday I pray and ask the Lord to change my life and the lives of my family in an eternal way in the services that day.

That is why the way I was feeling one Sunday evening surprised me so. I was tired, and I didn't want to go to church. My family and I had arrived at church early, so I sat in my car and I waited for the auditorium doors to open for the main service. I grabbed my Bible and began to read because I knew that I needed God to change my attitude.

I read a Psalm each morning along with some other chapters in my daily Bible reading. I turned to the next Psalm, the 82nd Psalm, and I began to read. I read the 83rd Psalm, then I began to read the 84th. There I received a sermon from my favorite Preacher, the Lord Himself, as I read: *"How amiable are* thy tabernacles, O LORD of hosts! My soul longeth, yea, even fainteth for the courts of the LORD: my heart and my flesh crieth out for the living God...Blessed are they that dwell in thy house: they will be still praising thee...For a day in thy courts is better than a thousand. I had rather be a doorkeeper in the house of my God, than to dwell in the tents of wickedness."

When I entered the doors of my church for service that evening, I determined not only to be faithful to church, but also to enter each service with enthusiasm and praise whether or not I was tired.

Faithfulness is a quality which God expects a wife to possess. He tells us in I Timothy 3:11 that a deacon's wife must be faithful, and I am sure God wishes that for every wife. But I Timothy 3:11 doesn't just say that a wife should be faithful to church. It bids her to be faithful in all things. The word *faithful* in my Webster's dictionary is defined as loyalty and nothing more. My Bible dictionary defines the word in this particular verse to mean *trustworthy and reliable*.

A wife is to be trustworthy, loyal, and reliable in all things. Allow me to share some areas in which a wife should be faithful.

1. A wife should be faithful to principles. Proverbs 1:8 says, "*My son, hear the instruction of thy father, and forsake not the law of thy mother.*" We are to be loyal to the good things which we have learned from our parents and our authorities. Not only should we not forsake the principles of right and wrong which we have been taught, but we should also cling to the principles of simple living.

For example, my mother is a very traditional woman. She is feminine, and she is a homemaker. When I was growing up at home, she often expressed concern about her youngest child. I was as different as night and day from my mother. I hated anything that had to do with homemaking, and I was slightly tomboyish. No two people could have seemed any more different.

I could have responded to these differences by throwing away all of the truths and things she had taught me while saying that because I cannot be like her, I may as well not try. This has been the typical attitude of my generation. We have said, "We cannot be stereotypical housewives. We can't be superwomen, so we may as well give ourselves a break. We have become so adept at giving ourselves a break that we have not only quit trying to be perfect, we have quit trying to do a good job at all. The world pokes fun at the woman of the 50's, while today's woman allows her home and family to fall apart before her very eyes. No problem with her as long as she can "find herself."

I am not a very great lady or a very great Christian, but I have tried to be faithful to all of the good things that my parents have taught me. I have tried to teach my children the traditions that my parents passed on to me. I am teaching my daughter to be feminine, to keep house, and to follow the traditions I have been taught. In doing so, my mother and I often laugh at the surprising similarities we have between us. Of course, I could never be as great as my mother, and I don't try. But I do try to be faithful to all of the good things I learned from her.

2. A wife should be faithful to people. My generation needs a revival of women who are faithful to love people just because they are "their people" or just because they once loved them. I have lived my life by this philosophy. When I make a commitment, I keep it. Such is the case with the commitment of my marriage vows. When I decide to love someone, I love them forever. If someone is a member of my family, I will always love that family member, and I will always be there for that family member to the best of my ability. If I once call someone my friend, that person will always be my friend no matter what happens.

These principles have hurt sometimes, but mostly, they have left me feeling happy, blessed, and satisfied. I have had friends who have not held to these same principles, and I have been asked how I handled it. My response to this question is as follows:

A. Love all your friends at all times regardless of their response to you.

B. If one friend is disloyal to another, be faithful to the friend who is your first priority. You may need to break fellowship with a friend, but you do not need to stop loving or being thoughtful.

C. Fill your time with fulfilling activities and uplifting thoughts so as to resist feeling self-pity.

D. Continue to trust your other friends as if you had never been betrayed.

E. Build a stronger relationship with the faithful One and take all those you love to Him in prayer.

The following is a poem I wrote expressing my love for Christ Who has been so faithful to me:

In our lives it's hard to know what friends will go or stay.
It's hard to know who'll stand by you and who will turn away.
The more we age, the more we find our friends choose different roads.
But there's Someone Who's always there to share each lonely load.
I will never leave nor forsake thee —
This promise grows much dearer every day.
Jesus Christ remains the same forever,
Just how He loved before He loves today.

Man and wife divide o'er things they think can't be forgiven;
Children grow and move away and parents go to Heaven.
But there's no time to hang our heads and murmur and complain,
Rejoice! You're in God's presence, in His presence you'll remain!

I will never leave nor forsake thee—
This promise grows much dearer every day.
Jesus Christ remains the same forever,
Just how He loved before He loves today.

REFRAIN:
He loved you so before, but He loves you so much more today.

In closing, allow me to ask you one more time as I end this chapter, "Are you qualified to be a wife?" And may I ask you this, "Have you been as faithful to 'your people' and to your friends as Jesus has been to you?"

Learning Compassion

The Ministry of Encouragement

Growing up in the home of a famous preacher to me was quite wonderful. I didn't have to grow very much before I realized that I was the daughter of a very special man. I realized from a young age that a lot of people loved me just because of who my parents were.

On the other hand, God and my parents had a way of keeping me humble. Most of all, my own weaknesses had a way of teaching me that I was no better than anyone else, even though God had placed me in a very special home. Why then did God place me in such a special home with two of His choicest servants if I was no better than anyone else? Even as a child, I understood (perhaps I was made to understand through wise teachers) that I was placed where I was for a very special purpose. I decided that purpose must be that of being an encouragement to my parents. I set about to do just that.

I rode home with my dad every Sunday morning, Sunday night, and Wednesday night after his appointment times at church. I sent him cards and notes when he left to go on his trips. I did whatever I could to be an encouragement to him. I must admit that there have been times when I was anything BUT an encouragement! So often when I meant to be an encouragement to my parents, they ended up drying my tears and being an encouragement to me. Still, I always thought and still believe that to be an encouragement is why God placed me where He did.

I also believe that encouragement is the main reason why God places every Christian lady where He places her. A husband and wife have two very different powers in their marriage. The husband's power is leadership. The wife's power is influence. If a wife wants to influence her husband, the best way to do this is through encouragement.

If we tell someone how to do something better, there is a small chance that they will listen to us. If we try to help someone to do something better through encouragement, there is a great chance that they will listen to us. A leader may sometimes have to lead in other ways, but an influencer can best influence through encouragement.

I often wonder what older ladies in our church will receive as a special award for the encouragement that they have given to the preacher. I believe we may find when we get to Heaven that some lady may have carried our preacher's ministry on the shoulders of her encouragement. Perhaps we will discover that just one little note strengthened our preacher and helped to sustain the ministry of First Baptist Church of Hammond, Indiana. I wish we all had enough faith to believe in what God could do with our little acts of encouragement.

I believe encouragement is important because I have experienced what it can do in my own life. The Lord has used little acts of encouragement to keep me going time and time again. If encouragement is so important, let us discuss some ways to practice it in our own lives.

Little Acts of Encouragement

1. Pray for a positive attitude. *"Rejoice in the Lord alway: and again I say, Rejoice."* (Philippians 4:4) Sometimes when I come to the Lord with a problem, I am unsure what to pray for. The older I get, the more I realize that problems are more complex than they seem and that I don't have the answers. I find myself asking the Lord to show me what to pray for. Time and time again, I have felt the Lord telling me to pray for a positive attitude. God has been so sweet to answer.

I am melancholy by nature. As a young girl, I loved stories that had a sad ending because I loved to cry at the end. (Men are usually quite baffled by our womanly desire to cry.) I even have to practice smiling sometimes because it is more natural for me to look angry. Yet if I have a pessimistic attitude, how in the world can God use me to be an encouragement to others?

I do not mean that we need to have a more positive attitude about ourselves. Rather, we need to develop a positive attitude about Christ and about all of His promises for our lives. In order to do this, we must think positively and we must talk positively. When we talk about the latest gossip, we develop pessimism. We must learn to take our burdens to the Lord in prayer and to leave them there until our next prayer time. *"Casting all your care upon him; for he careth for you."* (I Peter 5:7)

2. Replace negative comments with positive ones. If you are a complainer, I am not going to ask you to never complain again. Complaining is a difficult habit to break, and women are often experts at complaining. Instead, I would encourage you to make a positive comment every time you hear yourself complaining. Christian ladies today need to practice such statements as:

- "I just feel that everything is going to be all right."
- "I have a feeling that this is going to be the best year ever."
- "I just know that you are going to do a good job."

Rather, I am afraid that I am more prone to say:

- "What is going to happen next?"
- "Things couldn't get any worse, but I think they will anyway."

- "I hope you do okay and don't mess things up."

I think you would agree with me that these are not very encouraging statements. We need to practice making positive comments and to pray for victory over the sin of complaining.

3. Schedule a time in your week to do encouraging things for people. Perhaps you could get the prayer sheet from your church each week and just send a card to those who are sick or grieving. A lady in our church who has parents in bad health encourages people to send funny cards to her parents. This is a good idea. I do not mean that we should be inappropriate, but some get-well cards can be rather discouraging. Let's be uplifting in our encouragement and let's schedule time to do so.

4. Get a list of the favorite things of people whom you are trying to encourage. I believe that this practice is commonly known by people at Hyles-Anderson College and First Baptist Church, but it may not be practiced in some churches. For example, this list will give you ideas of how to be thoughtful without spending a lot of money. For example, if you are training a new soul winner, have a list of her favorite candy bars, flowers, colors, collectables, etc.

5. Learn to frequent dollar stores, thrift shops, and garage sales. These are places where even a person who doesn't have much money can afford to be a giver and an encourager. God can use even a small item to encourage others. All He really needs is a willing heart. In the Bible, God used small things like a rod, a few fish, and a few loaves of bread to do great things. In my life this past week, God has used a Kit-Kat candy bar, a box of Combo's (crackers), a single red rose, and a note to encourage me. The bearers of these simple gifts did not know it, but they carried me on the shoulders of their encouragement for a little while and helped me not to quit.

6. Make it a priority in your life to encourage God's ser-

vants, especially your preacher. I, for one, would like to be like the Shunamite woman who kept a place of encouragement available for the man of God, Elisha. (II Kings 4:8) Again, the tool that I use to encourage does not have to be much. It only needs to be given with a heart that is yielded to Christ. Then God will be able to do great things with it. As a preacher's daughter and now a preacher's wife, I have seen how God blesses those who encourage the preacher.

The melancholic side of me realizes that the problems of today are complex. The Bible says in John 16:33, "*...In the world ye shall have tribulation....*" That tribulation is expected to get worse until Jesus comes back again.

Yet that same verse says, "*...be of good cheer....*" Surely in a world of tribulation, it is important that God's work continues and prospers. If it is to prosper, God will use leaders to make it prosper. Leaders need followers who know how to be an encouragement. That's where the ladies come in. We are the experts at encouragement. I can't think of anything else I would rather be. Fundamentalism needs ladies who are of good cheer—ladies who have a positive attitude about Christ and His promises. We need ladies who will devote themselves to the ministry of encouragement and who will assure others that "everything is going to be all right."

Crybabies

"*When Jesus therefore saw her weeping, and the Jews also weeping which come with her, he groaned in the spirit, and was troubled, And said, Where have ye laid him? They said unto him, Lord, come and see. Jesus wept. Then said the Jews, Behold how he loved him!*" (John 11:33-36)

Though I do not in any way consider myself a sad person, I must admit that I am a crybaby. I tease my parents that I cried so often at the dinner table when I was a little girl that they quit even looking up from their food to see what was wrong.

My father was very wise and considerate in his handling of my tears. (I think this is because he was a crybaby, too!) When he would see me crying at the table, instead of asking me what was wrong in front of the family and embarrassing me, he would ask me to go into the kitchen and get him some iced tea. This gave me an excuse to get away from the crowded table and dry my eyes. Needless to say, my dad learned to drink a lot of iced tea.

As a five-year-old girl, my brother, sisters, and I were called to the platform by my father to speak a few words. Becky, Linda, and David did fairly well in their speeches. I stood by the microphone and cried.

When I was an eight-year-old girl, I saw my dad crying while I was sitting on his lap. He was crying for me. At that time I became a daddy's girl, and I don't think that my dad has shed too many tears in his life since that time that I have not cried with him, even though we may not have been together.

I often cried or at least fought back the tears when my

father cried during his preaching. I have often told my husband that I wish I was not such a crybaby. I tire of crying in front of thousands of people. Brother Schaap has always wisely admonished me never to feel badly about being a crybaby.

My husband was a crybaby, too! He cried almost every day on his way to school through the second grade. When Brother Schaap became a teenager, he tired of being a crybaby and asked God to take away his tears. God did that for a while, and Brother Schaap said it was one of the most miserable times of his life.

A few years ago, when my husband was preaching at a camp, he discovered that a 12-year-old girl at the camp had become pregnant by her mother's boyfriend. Brother Schaap said that he was so frustrated at being unable to help this little girl that he threw himself across the bed of his cabin and cried and cried and cried. When my husband shared the story with me, I thought to myself, "What good did that do?" Pretty foolish question coming from a fellow crybaby!

Sometime after, I learned what good it can do to simply cry for someone else. Our church had entered into another heated attack. Some people had said some things that were not only untrue, but also insane and very hurtful. This time not a few people were falsely incriminated, but thousands. I was one of those thousands of people who was hurting. A special friend spoke to me and asked me how I was doing. I answered that I was doing okay. Then my friend began to cry and cry and cry. I don't consider my friend a crybaby, so I asked her why she was crying. She said that she just couldn't stand to see me hurt any more. In other words, my friend was crying for me. She did not take away the hurt; she did not clear anyone's name or reputation; she did not give me a gift or money. She just cried. I felt better somehow and felt like I had been given one of the finest gifts that I had been given in a long time.

This special token of love and friendship brought my mind back to John chapter eleven where we are told that *"Jesus wept."* Could it be that Jesus is a crybaby, too? I think not! Jesus is like my friend in this way. John 11:33 tells us that He knew that Mary was hurting. He saw her crying and the Jews crying with her, and He, too, began to cry. When I read this story several weeks ago, I was startled and encouraged with a thought which I had never had before.

Many times I have read passages in the Bible like Isaiah 38:5 which says, *"...I have heard thy prayer, I have seen thy tears."* I have even read in Psalm 56:8 that my tears are bottled up in Heaven. (What a big bottle for a crybaby like me!) Yet I had never before realized that sometimes Jesus actually cries with us when we cry. I am not sure that He always cries when we do, but I do believe there are specific times when He actually does cry with us. He cried with Mary over the death of her loved one. Perhaps this is one of those times when Jesus doesn't just see our tears, but this is one of those times when He cries with us.

In April of 1993, Mrs. Ray Young lost her father in death just days after I had been reading John chapter 11. I saw Debi crying at the funeral and in church the Sunday afterward. I cried with her and was comforted to believe that Jesus was crying with her also.

Why did Jesus cry in John chapter 11? He cried not only because when Mary hurt, He hurt; but also He cried to show how much he loved Lazarus. The verse directly after *"Jesus wept"* says this, *"Then said the Jews, Behold how he loved him!"* Jesus cried to show others his love. My dad cried for me when I was a little girl. I understood his love and became a daddy's girl. My friend cried for me, and I understood that she loved me. I received the strength I needed to continue on in a time of trial. Sooooo...being a crybaby is not so bad after all. Allow

me to share with you some thoughts about this:

1. Tears are an ultimate expression of love.

2. Tears are an ultimate teaching tool.

3. Every Christian, especially one who teaches others, should pray for the Lord to give him tears. Singers who cry, preachers who cry will have extra passion and compassion in their singing and in their preaching.

4. Every wife, parent, grandparent, etc. should pray for the ability to cry for others. This is a hard prayer to pray because every time I cry for a person, I usually cry because I have been through something difficult which causes me to, in part, understand their hurt. In order to be crybabies, we must allow God to break our hearts. This is painful, but rewarding, as we are able to reach people through our tears.

So I thank you, friend, for your tears which you shared with me the other day. I thank You, Jesus, that You not only see my tears, but sometimes, I believe, You cry with me. One more thing, Lord—thanks a lot for making me a crybaby. In that respect, I hope I never change!

When Christians Are Hurting

*A*s a child I was afraid of people who were hurting. I ran away from the one-eyed man in our church, even though he often carried candy in his pocket. I even got a little nervous being around someone who walked with crutches. My childish mind did not understand the nature of their affliction, and therefore, I did not wish to deal with it.

I am afraid as an adult I have often reacted in the same way. That is to say that I have not wished to deal with people who were afflicted or hurting because I did not understand the nature of their affliction.

Several years ago, a lady who had lost a young son in a car accident spoke in a meeting that I attended about how to deal with those who are hurting. Her talk helped to answer some of the questions that I had about those who are sick, dying, or grieving. Allow me to share with you my questions and her answers.

1. Is it proper to mention a loved one who has passed away to someone who is grieving? YES! People wish more than anything to talk about their departed loved one. When we feel awkward about mentioning them, we cause the grieving to feel that their loved one has died all over again.

Let me also mention that I believe it is good and proper to mention someone who is wayward or backslidden to their parents or to a loved one. When fellow Christians cease to mention a wayward child to his parents, we can unknowingly make the hurting parents to feel like their child has died.

How we mention a wayward child is important. For example, if we ask, "How is so-and-so?", we may catch the parents off guard or cause them to feel that we are trying to get the latest gossip. If we mention some fond memory we have of the loved one, whether he be dead or just sick or wayward, we encourage the hurting loved one. When we mention some good influence the person has had on our lives or someone else's, we emphasize the worth of the parents and of their child.

2. Is it proper to ask people who are hurting to give an account of their accident or illness? YES! When I am talking to people who have been through some sort of tragedy, I ask them questions about it because I understand their need to talk about what they are going through. I always preface my questions with, "I know you may have been asked this several times, and if you do not wish to talk about it, I understand." This gives the persons an "out" if they just do not feel like talking. However, nine times out of ten, those persons who are sick or grieving have been alone with their thoughts a lot, and they need to discuss their experiences with another human being.

Of course, if the person who is hurting is going through a divorce or the grief of a wayward child, it probably would not be proper to ask him for the latest account. However, to say to the hurting loved one, "I know you are hurting right now," is perfectly proper. Unfortunately, it is often the opportunist who asks those who are hurting to give an account of their struggles. This type of person merely wants to hear the latest trash. On the other hand, good and godly people often avoid Christians who are hurting because they do not want to appear nosy or curious. It is the fellowship of good and godly people that is needed most when people are hurting. Because of this, I believe it is not only proper, but also good for a Christian to say to his brother, "I'm sorry this happened. I am praying for you." Ask the Lord to reveal to your hurting sister in Christ that your motives are sincere, and He will.

3. Should I extend some pity? ABSOLUTELY NOT! Hurting Christians, especially men, do not want your pity. Rather, they wish to have your encouragement and your patience.

4. Should I say, "I know how you feel"? NO! The truth is you do not understand how they feel. (In order to put things where we can reach them, let me give an example from years ago when my father endured severe persecution. I did not understand how it felt to be a staff member at First Baptist Church and to have your preacher with whom you had worked 20 or 30 years go through persecution. Those staff members did not know how it felt to be Cindy Schaap and to have a dad undergo persecution such as my dad had. I did not know how it felt to be Mrs. Jack Hyles and to have my husband undergoing persecution. I did not understand how it felt to be Dr. Jack Hyles and to be the man undergoing persecution.)

However, I do think it is sometimes helpful to share with someone who is hurting something you have gone through which may have been similar. At the time of my father's persecution, one of the newest members of First Baptist Church was a preacher's daughter whose dad had undergone severe persecution. While I did not understand how she felt and she did not understand how I felt, her account of her experiences was comforting to me. We did not sit for hours sharing a pity party. That would not have been a help to either of us. She shared a few moments with me and, though she did not realize it, she was a great comfort.

5. Should I always remain positive with the person who is hurting? NOT ALWAYS! While it is good to be positive with people who are hurting, we should also make them feel that we understand that they will be hurting and that we realize that is okay. The truth is that it does hurt when someone is sick or dying; it does hurt when a loved one is struggling in their marriage; and it does hurt when a friend has betrayed us. That hurt will probably cause us to feel every negative emotion that there is to feel. We do not have to give in to those emotions and let them into our hearts, but we will feel them. I am sure that Jesus felt a lot of emotions when He was tempted in the wilderness, but He did not give in to them. That is the difference.

6. If I know something negative that was said or written about someone, should I share it with that person or his loved ones? NO, unless there is something that they can or should do in reaction to what has been said or written. As the daughter of a man who endured a lot of persecution, I tried not to read or know the negative things that were said or written. Though I have felt bitterness, I do not want to let it into my heart. I prevent this from happening by shielding myself as much as possible from bad news.

7. What if I simply cannot understand the behavior of the person who is hurting? BE PATIENT! As stated earlier, a person who is hurting will go through every emotion there is. I know in my own experience with hurt that I have become shy and awkward in situations in which I would have usually felt comfortable. I have seemed, I'm sure, to be angry when I was just preoccupied or embarrassed. Remember that when someone slings mud at a person, that person is going to feel dirty, no matter how pure their lifestyle might be.

Because of this, we need to be more patient, and we need to be sweeter and more attentive when a Christian is hurting. We also need to realize that any person we meet today might be hurting, no matter how put together and calm they may appear to be. Perhaps we should just be a little sweeter and a little more patient with everyone with whom we come in contact.

Let me also give some word of advice to Christians who are

the ones who are hurting right now. Be patient with your brothers and sisters in Christ who do not understand your grief. All of us have experienced different levels of suffering. Our ability to relate with others in their suffering is related to our own experience. This does not have to be the case, but most of the time it is.

I myself feel that I have just graduated from the first grade when it comes to dealing with the suffering of others. I am ashamed when I realize the number of people whom I have "let down" when they were hurting. However, I can keep growing in my ability to be a comfort to others. I find that if I am going to comfort others, I must be there for them, even if it is only for a few minutes a week. I must send them notes of encouragement and, most of all, I must schedule time to do it. Most people do not comfort others because they do not realize the importance of comforting. When they realize the importance of comforting, they will schedule it into their lives just like Bible reading, eating, sleeping, etc.

Let's also remember that Christian leaders carry burdens on their shoulders all the time that are like the ones that we just bear once in awhile. Because of this, we need to always be extra patient and loving with them.

Let me encourage the hurting Christian also to find comfort in the Lord. Do not try to find comfort in someone of the opposite sex and be careful in giving it. I have found a lot of comfort in my husband. There have been things that I could only discuss with him, and it has brought a special uniqueness to our marriage. However, I have learned that I can be a hindrance to my husband's ministry if I take all my problems to him. Because of this, there are many things that I now only discuss with the Lord. What a blessed experience this has been!

The Bible tells us that Jesus' *"compassions fail not."* He never fails to notice when a Christian is hurting. He never leaves a kind word unspoken or gets impatient with our varying emotions. He always does the appropriate comforting deed at the appropriate time. Unfortunately, we cannot be just like Him until we see Him some day, but that doesn't mean we cannot try. Let's be more like Jesus when Christians are hurting.

When Christians Are Straying

As a teenager and as a very young adult, I classified people into basically one of two groups: those who were "jerks" and those who were not "jerks." Of course, what category a person fit into was based solely on my opinion. Those who were classified as "jerks" were not going to get any sympathy or attention from me.

Now that I am a little bit older, I have had to broaden my system of classification just a little because I have done some pretty "jerky" things myself. I have also been surprised by what "jerky" things can be done by friends and those who come to me for counsel. I only had to do a little bit of counseling to realize that I needed help in my attitude towards Christians who stray out of the desirable category and into the undesirable. I still do not have all the answers about how to deal with Christians when they stray from what we find to be Biblically-acceptable behavior, but I have found some truths that have been extremely helpful to me. Allow me to share them with you.

During my devotions one morning several years ago, I stumbled upon Proverbs 14:16. "*A wise man feareth, and departeth from evil: but the fool rageth, and is confident.*" I have no doubt that this verse can be interpreted in ways other than the way that I have interpreted it, but I am sure that the Lord drew my attention to this verse to teach me how to react to Christians who are straying.

Proverbs 14:16 teaches me the difference between the way a fool reacts to sin and the way a wise man reacts to sin, whether it be his own sin or the sins of others. I would like to apply it to our reaction to the sins of others.

A Fool's Reactions

First of all, there are two reactions that a fool has when he hears of another's sin.

1. The fool rages or becomes angry. Since I do not wish to be a fool, I do not wish to rage when I discover the sins of others.

2. The fool feels confident. Again, since I do not wish to be a fool, I cannot react to another's sins with the "I-would-never-do-such-a-thing" attitude.

A Wise Person's Reactions

This verse tells me two things that a wise man does when he hears of another's sin.

1. The wise man fears. Since I wish to react wisely to the sins of another, I must not say, "I would never do such a thing," but rather, "It could have been me." Of course, we all have a choice, and we have the power through Christ to do that which is right in any situation. Still, I think the Bible is teaching that it is wise to have a proper fear of sin. Without Christ's help, any of us could be sin's next victim.

2. The wise man departs from evil. A wise man reacts to the sins of others not only by saying, "It could have been me," or fearing the sin, but also by departing from it. That is, we should ask ourselves what we can do to avoid making the same mistake. There are not always standard answers as to why one Christian goes astray and another does not. However, we can evaluate in our minds why a Christian has strayed, and we can set up principles that will help us to avoid making the same mistakes. The longer I live, the more I believe that the biggest difference between righteous and unrighteous people is the habits and the principles by which they live. We are all made of the same flesh, and we have the same temptations. The wise man, however, has scheduled his habits in such a way that when temptation comes, it is much harder for him to fall than it would be for others. I think it would be wise for all of us to make a list with pen and paper of what we are going to do to avoid some of the pitfalls the Devil enjoys putting in the Christian's pathway. Let me share a few other ideas that have helped me in dealing with Christians who are straying.

1. Give the Christian who strays to the Lord. I am the type of Christian who likes to fix things myself, and I like to fix them right away. Because of this, I am tempted to go straight to a Christian who is straying and tell her what I think of her "jerky" behavior. Do you know what I have discovered? When we lecture or scold a straying Christian when the Holy Spirit has not given us the authority to do so, we would be equally as helpful if we just beat on a tin can with a spoon. There is nothing we can do to change a person who is closed to the workings of the Holy Spirit, no matter how eloquent our speech. I am learning to leave the hard preaching to the God-called preachers and not to take matters into my own hands.

Instead, when I hear a report about a Christian which causes me to grieve, I officially give that person to the Lord. The Lord seems to ask me sometimes, "Cindy, do you trust Me with so-and-so?" I am tempted to answer, "Of course, Lord, but wouldn't You like just a little bit of my help?" Yet I have found the Lord works His best when I finally take my hands off. When I trust Him with my best students, my best friends, and loved ones, I am demonstrating my faith.

2. Give the Christian who strays a scheduled time in your life. I realize that it would be impossible to include a scheduled time for every straying Christian with whom we are acquainted. However, when the Lord calls you to help a particular Christian or a Christian for whom you are responsible, it is best to schedule the time that you will spend helping her, praying for her, and thinking about her. I do not believe that we should walk around worried and depressed 100% of the time just because we are concerned about a particular Christian. This will cause us to become ineffective as wives, mothers, etc.

The first time I counseled with a woman who had serious marriage problems, I drove home feeling nauseous, and I wondered how I was going to be able to function normally with my family that evening. I learned quickly that the spiritual problems of others are not something that you can allow to enter into every part of your life, no matter how important those people may be to you.

3. Give the Christian who strays your unconditional love. When I was about 15 years old, I got suspended from school for one day. I must say that I was not right with the Lord, and I deserved to be suspended from school. I spent most of my day of suspension at a park near my house praying and reading a book which was entitled, *I Hate Myself.* The book was about self-esteem, and I do not remember a thing that it taught, but I do remember that the title expressed exactly how I was feeling about myself at the time.

I try to remember that day when I am counseling someone who has failed miserably in her Christian life. Most Christians who are straying hate themselves for their behavior. They generally act cocky and self-assured which causes us to want to give them a swift kick in the seat of the pants. Some of them need just that, but many will fall down and never get back up if we treat them the way our flesh tells us to treat them. As I recall my own failures as a Christian, I realize that a Christian who strays probably needs three things: (1) love, (2) someone to give him a reason why he should get back up, and (3) someone to tell him how he can get back up.

When I was suspended from school, I feared my parent's reaction. My parents gave the three needs that I mentioned in the previous paragraph. They gave me love, and they told me why I should get back up. I had gotten suspended for defending a student I thought was being mistreated by a teacher. The problem was that I had done that defending in a disrespectful manner.

My dad reacted to the situation by telling me that he liked the fact that I was compassionate toward the Lord and toward others. This reaction gave me a why for getting back up. I had something to offer the Lord, and my dad pointed this out to me. My parents also told me how to get back up. My dad said something like this: "Cindy, you have one basic problem. You need to learn when to keep your mouth shut."

After I learned that my dad still loved me and after he pointed out the fact that he even liked me by expressing something good he saw in me, I was ready to take his admonition. His admonition was simple and uncomplicated. He gave me only one problem to solve. I am sure that there were many other problems that needed to be solved in my life that day. However, I needed one simple prescription; I couldn't have handled much more than that.

If my parents never did anything else for me in my life, I would forever be indebted to them for being there when I hated myself. The average Christian who is straying is not easy to love. They act like they know it all and they have no need for anyone, but inside they are probably hating themselves. If we can be there for them now, they will never forget.

I don't remember all of what my parents said to me in family altar when I was growing up, but the words they spoke when I was down are forever etched in my heart.

4. Ask the Lord to bring the Christian who strays to where He wants her to be. I pray every day that my children will be what I hope they will be. I ask the Lord to make them honest, pure, loving, thoughtful, forgiving, and so forth. One day as I was praying, the Lord seemed to say, "Cindy, you're asking me to make them perfect." Since then, I add these words to the long list of virtues which I hope for them to have: "Lord help me to accept them the way they are."

My desire for all Christian loved ones is that they will have my standards and my convictions because I believe they are Bible standards. My desire is that they will continue on the road of God's will and never detour to the right or to the left. If they do take a detour, it is my prayer that they will be right back on track tomorrow. In my own life, I have discovered that God does not always fix things today or even tomorrow. His work in others' lives is often unique compared to His work in my own life. I no longer ask the Lord to make them all that I wish them to be, but rather I ask Him to bring them to where He wishes them to be.

I was telling a friend the other day about some of the mistakes I had made growing up as Jack Hyles' daughter. I told her about my suspension from school. My friend's response was, "You're lucky! You made your mistakes when you were young and those mistakes did not have such bitter consequences." I wept when my friend left, and I thanked the Lord for His mercy to me. I also asked Him to help me to be more loving when Christians are straying.

Put It in the Headlines!

All of us have felt the frustration in recent years of bad reporting. I have a hard time understanding why the press finds it so difficult to report the truth. It is a mystery to me why they are so intent upon reporting bad news while leaving out so much good. I find myself reading the newspaper and watching the television news less and less. Yet when I'm standing in the grocery line and see people buying copies of newspapers which have such unbelievable headlines as this: "Three-year-old girl gives birth to sixty-pound baby," I am reminded that the press is not the entire problem. The problem is with the public and what it likes to hear. The problem is with me. I am, after all, part of the public, and though I did not buy the previously referred to newspaper, I did read the headline with a lot of disbelief and a little bit of interest. The press is simply writing what they have learned people like to hear—bad news, whether or not it is true.

While we fuss about the press and its lack of accountability, we need to realize that we are all reporters in one way or another. We need to ask ourselves if we are doing any better at reporting what is right and good than those who are paid to do so. Several years ago while at a Youth Conference in Missouri, I heard Dr. Bob Gray from Longview, Texas, preach a sermon from I Corinthians 14:24 which says, *"But if all prophesy, and there come in one that believeth not, or one unlearned, he is convinced of all, he is judged of all."* This sermon changed my life in an unusual way. I realized that when someone who is unsaved or ignorant about God's Word enters a church where the Word of God is being preached, his opinion about what is being preached will not only be formed by the preacher himself, but also by all those present. In other words, every church member, even a lady, is in some way a preacher or a reporter to the visitors who come to church. Ladies, let me ask you a question. What kind of reporter are you?

If I had visited your church last Sunday and watched your reporting, what would my opinion have been after the sermon was finished? Would I have been more convinced of the truths of the sermon because I had watched you or less convinced? If my opinion of your pastor and your church were to be formed by watching (or hearing) your reporting, what would my opinion be?

What if I heard something bad about your husband and then watched your reporting to see if it were true? What would I see expressed in your eyes about his character? What would the words you speak and the inflections of your voice tell me? You may say, "Well, people are going to believe what they want to believe anyway." Yes, I suppose this is true, but all people must look somewhere to form their opinions. It was actually a very wonderful day in my life when I realized how important it was that my reporting be a report of what is good and of what is true. Please allow me to share with you some ideas about how you can be a good reporter as a church member, as a wife, and in any role you might find yourself.

1. Be a good reporter with your smile. Have you ever noticed how the facial expressions of a reporter can affect our belief about what he is saying? If I watched your facial expressions, what kind of a report would they give me? Does your facial expression in church report good of your pastor and his message? Does your facial expression when you are around your husband or your loved ones report good about your feelings about them?

My mother has a natural and beautiful smile while I do not. When I am sitting still and listening, I look like I have just eaten a dill pickle. In fact, when I was a student at Hyles-Anderson College, there were a few students who would shout, "Smile! God loves you!" when they would pass me in the hallway. My inward response was, "Shut up!"

Then one day God did a wonderful thing in my life. He convinced me that my smile was important. He showed me that if He could use five loaves and two fishes to feed five thousand people, He could do great things with simply a smile.

I began to practice smiling! I was too shy to practice in public, so I practiced at home. I literally plastered a huge smile on my face and kept it there while I was alone vacuuming, cleaning the house, and so forth. You may say, "How silly!" My response is, "Try it. It works." I still may look like I've eaten a dill pickle sometimes. (I am, after all, a crybaby as I told you in the previous chapter.) But I want to have a smile that God can use to do some good reporting. There are a few folks to whom I purposely do not look when I want to see a smile, because I know it will not be there. God forbid that I should be one of those people!

How I look at my husband has always been important to me. If I am to demonstrate Christ and His love for the church to others through my marriage, surely I had better learn to look at him with respect and with a smile! How I look at my children is important! I remember Jaclynn telling me when she was a little girl, "Mom, she is a very good baby sitter because she smiles a lot."

2. Be a good reporter by sitting toward the front of the church. Of course, not everyone can sit in the front of any church, especially not in ours. For many years I sat on the very back row with an elderly lady whom I loved like a grandmother. When my husband decided we should sit toward the front,

I gladly obliged. I was learning, after all, that where I sat gave a certain report, and I wanted it to be a good one. I wanted the report to be true which was this: "I love my church and my pastor. I love to hear his good preaching." Report your love for your husband by sitting by his side in church and in the car. People are watching, and they need to receive a clear, true and good message. Good reporting about a marriage will keep a lot of the wrong type of women away.

3. Be a good reporter by walking the aisle in church. I have walked the aisle quite regularly since I was a little girl. I am not saying I do it to make a statement. I walk the aisle because God is working in my heart. In fact, there have been times when God has told me to walk the aisle and I have not. I then have struggled in my Christian life the following week and have known it was because I did not walk the aisle when I should have.

I was in a youth meeting several years ago where a pastor's wife walked the aisle during the invitation. It was several minutes into the invitation and very few teenagers had walked the aisle.

I noticed as soon as she walked the aisle, the invitation "broke open," and scores of young people went forward. Many great decisions were made. I decided then that I would not hesitate to follow God's leading even when He led me down the aisle during my husband's preaching. I began to believe that God could use my example in this area to do great things for Himself. Be a good reporter of your love for your husband by walking respectfully when you are walking with him. Do not rush ahead of him or lag behind him. Be aware of his lead and walk at his side.

4. Be a good reporter by shaking your head when you listen to your pastor. While you are vacuuming and practicing that smile, also practice shaking your head and saying things such as, "Honey, I am sure you made the right decision," or "Pastor, your sermon was just right today. I know you will make the right decision about that particular problem. I'll be praying for you." I've seen some churches where the ladies wave their hankies to show their support for their pastor. I suppose this "dill pickle eater" is not ready for that, but I enjoy watching their reporting and have found it to be good.

I have learned that my role as a pastor's daughter and now as a pastor's wife is not a role to use to report problems or to report what I did not like. (It was a hard lesson for me to learn, believe me.)

My role is to pray and to encourage. People who are always reporting problems show, most of all, their lack of faith that God can take care of it through their prayers. I am not saying that a church member or a wife should never report big problems to a leader, but we should not make a career out of it.

5. Be a good reporter by singing and by praising. If I watched you singing a song in church, would I be convinced that the words were true? God made us to bring praise to Him! Surely we should be good reporters in our songs of praise. Report your love to God, to your church, and to your husband by speaking only words of praise about them. It would be sad to think that bad reports about our husbands could be substantiated by our own words and attitudes.

These are very practical ideas and areas in which this writer has definitely not arrived. I am probably not even in first grade when it comes to reporting skills.

Sometimes, I have even rebelled against the fact that my family is in the public eye and that others are watching me and listening to me. One day, however, I realized what an opportunity God had given me. I have the opportunity to report good and truth about God Himself and about those I love. Yet God doesn't need someone in the public eye to report His truth.

He'll use any lady who believes He can use her.

So watch me, world! Listen to what I have to say! I have some very good news to report, and I have some wonderful truths to share! The truth is this: "I love God, my church, my pastor, my husband, and my family very, very much! Put it in the headlines!"

How Not to Quit Soul Winning

As a wife and mother of young children, I realized that there were many ways that the Devil can try to keep a lady from soul winning. As a matter of fact, the Devil tries to keep me from doing a lot of things. Each semester when I began teaching a new class of girls at Hyles-Anderson College on the subject, "The Christian Wife," I would find myself in the middle of an onslaught of temptation, especially in the early morning hours of the days I was going to teach. I would often find myself tested and tried in the exact area that I would be teaching about that particular day. Things went wrong that normally would go smoothly, and I'd get the feeling that the Devil just did not want me to teach.

Oftentimes, when my husband and I are scheduled to speak at a certain Youth Conference or when he is speaking at a particular church meeting, I feel a certain type of pressure that reminds me that the Devil would really like to destroy our efforts. I find this type of pressure somewhat flattering. My husband and I have often said to each other that the surest sign that the Lord wants to use us is in the persistence the Devil shows in disrupting our lives. However, I also take the devil's havoc seriously and have had to seek the Lord diligently to find deliverance from the Devil's wiles.

Looking back on my life thus far, I am amazed at the fact that there is a time that the Devil fights me more than any other time. He does not fight me the most when I am going to teach the Lord's choicest ladies. Nor does he fight me the most when I am going to speak somewhere. Rather, he fights me most when I am planning to go soul winning. This tells me that soul winning is probably the activity I do in my Christian service which the Devil hates the most. I think any lady who has even thought about going soul winning has experienced some of the temptations to give up about which I am talking. Because of this, I would like to share with you six things I have learned that have helped me not to quit soul winning.

1. Realize the significance of every simple prayer. I believe that every time I pray, God does something in response to my prayer. I try to stay in touch with the Lord throughout the week so I do not need to get "prayed up" when I am going soul winning. Sometimes, I may spend extra time in prayer for my soul-winning time, and I prefer praying on my knees because it shows my reverence to God. However, I believe that even when I do not have that extra bit of time to spend with the Lord and even when I am praying in the car on my way to go soul winning, God will still respond to my prayer.

This type of belief not only encourages me to pray more, while the "God-can't-bless-me-because-I-didn't-pray-enough" attitude only encourages me to pray less and to want to quit soul winning.

There are some times when I go soul winning, and God's answer to my prayers are quite evident. One week my husband and I were speaking at a Youth Conference in Greenville, Michigan, and I took some of the teens out soul winning. A teenage girl named Kim and I went to visit a teenage prospect named Nicole. Kim had been to visit Nicole before and warned me that her dad was mean and scary. I knocked on the door, and guess who answered? It was the mean and scary dad. He got sweetly saved in a matter of minutes, and Kim was in shock. I saw three other parents of teenage prospects saved that day, and I had no trouble believing that God had answered my prayer.

However, a few weeks before I had stopped to witness to a college-age girl who didn't look mean and scary at all—but she was! I asked her if she died today would she go to Heaven. She proceeded to tell me that it was none of my business, and she didn't tell me very kindly. In fact, she was as rude as she could possibly be. I didn't win anyone to the Lord that day, and yet I believe the Lord used me in as great a way that day as He did that Saturday in Greenville, Michigan. Why? Because I asked Him to. I must believe that way, or else I will be discouraged and will not go soul winning next time.

I believe the most common reason that ladies quit soul winning (or never start) is because they believe that great salvation experiences can only happen to mystical ladies who are better soul winners or better prayer warriors than they are. The Bible tells me in Luke 11:9, *"And I say unto you, Ask, and it shall be given you; seek, and ye shall find; knock, and it shall be opened unto you."*

I believe the secret to being a consistent soul winner is the same as the secret to getting saved. That is simple faith in what God can and will do with a simple prayer, even though we may not see it right away. I believe that when I get to Heaven I will rejoice with those adults whom I saw saved that Saturday in Greenville, Michigan. I am also looking forward to seeing how He used me on the week when I didn't see anyone saved, because I do believe He did something great that day. I must believe He did something great that day. I must believe that or I will quit soul winning.

Also, let me say that a soul winner should be more specific in her prayers to the Lord. In my own personal walk with the Lord, I have found that He answers my prayers more if they are specific. Therefore, instead of asking the Lord to bless my soul winning, I would ask Him more specifically to give me more boldness about speaking up in public places and a more positive attitude about the results of my soul winning. I pray specif-ically about these things because these are areas where I need particular help. The more specific I am about my needs, the more the Lord seems to answer.

2. Go soul winning so that you may give, expecting nothing in return. Mrs. JoBeth Hooker spoke in our Phoster Club on the verses found in Luke 6:33-34. *"And if ye do good to them which do good to you, what thank have ye? for sinners also do even the same. And if ye lend to them of whom ye hope to receive, what thank have ye? for sinners also lend to sinners, to receive as much again."* Mrs. Hooker's talk and these verses encouraged me to go soul winning expecting nothing in return. Many peo-ple go soul winning so that they can receive the blessings that they have heard others tell about. If they do not receive those blessings, the Devil tells them that they must not have been qualified, and they quit.

I think sometimes the Lord allows us to go through times when we do not see the fruit of our labors because He wants to see if we will still give of ourselves, even when we receive noth-ing in return. Again, I believe that the Lord is always doing great things through the soul winner who is asking and going. However, we may not always see what He is doing. If we go soul winning expecting nothing in return, such as instant gratifica-tion or an amazing story to tell, we will keep going soul winning even during those "dry periods" of our lives.

3. Thank the Lord on the way home for every soul-win-ning experience you have had that day. This little ritual has helped me in developing the faith I need to be persistent as a soul winner. I thank the Lord in the car on the way home from soul winning for every experience I had that day. Let me give you an example.

One Sunday, I took a heart-shaped Valentine box of candy to one of my new converts. That new convert had promised me she would go to church with me that Sunday. When I got to the door, she willingly took the candy I had brought her and then informed me that she would not be able to go to church with me after all. She gave me what I call "the-don't-call-me, I'll-call-you" speech. I could have gone home from soul winning discouraged that day. I was five dollars poorer and, seemingly, for no good reason. However, I cannot afford to get discouraged about something as important as soul winning. Because of this, I thanked the Lord for the privilege of giving that candy to my new convert. I believe that the Lord will use that deed because I asked Him to do so. If I never see how He uses it, I still had the privilege of doing something kind "unto the least of one of these," thereby giving to the Lord. If I never see the reward of my effort, then I have had the privilege of giving, expecting nothing in return.

When I have what I would call an unusually good day, I thank the Lord for that. The Devil puts enough temptation in my way as a soul winner that I have learned to savor every blessing that Jesus sends my way. The longer I rejoice in the conversions, the easier it is for me to keep going. I like to think about what it may be like in Heaven when a sinner gets saved. I imagine that the angels quit playing tag every time I win someone because they want to see redemption one more time. This type of thinking keeps me excited about soul winning.

4. **Go soul winning to be an encouragement to other Christians.** The Phoster Club is a soul-winning ministry in our church. It is a trainer/trainee system of soul winning. It is difficult for a trainer to miss Phoster Club because they know their trainees are counting on them. More people drop out of Phoster Club at the trainee stage than the trainer stage. Why? Because they do not think anyone is counting on them for encouragement.

However, they are wrong. Trainers need encouragement as

well as trainees. In fact, I believe that the main difference between trainers and trainees is that the trainer has learned how to fake that she is not afraid. We all have certain fears about soul winning, and we need each other. We should go soul winning (whether we are experienced soul winners or the new kids on the block) with the thought in mind that we are there to encourage others. It is then we will realize the importance of our faithfulness. We will also not make such statements as, "I don't think she really meant that when she prayed," or "We sure are having a bad day today." Soul winners who are negative in their attitudes and discourage others seldom stay soul winners for long.

5. Go soul winning in order to gain wisdom. Proverbs 11:30 says, "*...and he that winneth souls is wise.*" This verse also has motivated me to be a soul winner through the years. I need wisdom to rear my children as well as to do many other things, and I am trusting the Lord to give it to me because I am asking Him for it and because I am a soul winner.

6. Go soul winning with the right motive. For many years I was motivated to go soul winning and to do many things to please my parents. I believe this is a good motive. However, I know of some adult children who have been terribly let down by their Christian parents who chose a life of sin after many years of serving the Lord full time. Because of this, I realize that to go soul winning just because I love my parents is not good enough. In fact, any motivation for soul winning other than love for Christ is not good enough either.

James 1:12 is a very special verse to me which says, "*Blessed is the man that endureth temptation:* (perhaps the temptation to quit soul winning) *for when he is tried, he shall receive the crown of life, which the Lord hath promised to them that love him.*" I don't know what the word *endure* means in the Greek, but it reminds me of something I do at the dentist. God seems to be promising us a reward, not for going on victoriously for the Lord, but rather just for going on. But He also says that the reward will go to those who love Him. Why? Because the only people who will keep on serving the Lord (soul winning) no matter what happens are those who are motivated by love for Jesus Christ. I don't suppose any of us can measure how pure our motives for soul winning are. However, we can get to know our Lord better all the time so that we can learn to love Him more. We can ask Him to teach us to love Him more, and we can ask Him to help us serve Him because we love Him.

I am not the best soul winner who ever walked the halls of First Baptist Church of Hammond, Indiana, nor do I come close to being that. However, I have been a soul winner since I was eleven years old on a pretty consistent basis. I also have been tempted to quit as often as anyone else, I'm sure. Because of this, it is my privilege to share with you some tried and proven methods from my own experience about how to keep on soul winning. Let's not quit, or perhaps I should say for some of you, let's start going soul winning.

Dealing with Temptation

Temptations Women Face

$\mathcal{L}uke$ 4:1-14 gives my favorite account of the temptation of Jesus. The Bible says in Luke 4:1 that the Holy Spirit led Jesus into temptation at a time when he was Spirit-filled. This proves that a woman can be a Spirit-filled Christian and still go through great temptation.

I have been through seasons of temptation during my life. In fact, looking back, it seems as if each season of life has had a temptation with a different face.

During my childhood, I was faced with the temptation to accept or reject salvation; I chose to accept it.

During my teen years, I was tempted with several things. I was tempted with rebellion, especially during my freshman and sophomore years of high school. I was tempted to follow my own will instead of God's will. I was tempted to date and marry the wrong person and to compromise my dating standards. Surely the teen years are a season of great temptation.

During my twenties, I was tempted to follow a different path than the one my parents and pastor had taught me from childhood.

During my thirties, I faced my greatest temptation, and I faced a few years of my own "wilderness experience." I have no major regrets or "skid-row" stories to tell from this era, but it was a season of spiritual oppression for me.

During my first year in my forties, I found myself asking the question, "Do I really want to go any further in my service for Christ?" My answer is "Yes!" I want to go as far as is the Lord's will for me. Yet I hear the voice of temptation in my ear saying,

"Just say no!" I feel tempted to quit and to live for self.

If you think with me and look back on your life, I believe you will realize that all of life is full of seasons of temptation. I Corinthians 10:13 says, *"There hath no temptation taken you but such as is common to man...."* Perhaps if we compared our lives, we might discover that each decade has brought us temptations which are common with each other. Our circumstances would surely be different, but the temptations are probably the same.

The older I get, the more I find great comfort in the thought that I am not in this alone. The world does have some good ideas with their support groups, but they are missing the Person and the Book which are the Rock and Fortress of any support group.

For the next few chapters, I want to share with you some thoughts from Luke 4 about temptations that women face. I want you to allow me to be your support to aid in whatever temptation you might be facing. Better yet, I want to bring you support from Jesus and from the Bible, which has been a particular help to me.

In the first chapter, I just want to console you by saying that whatever you are facing, you are not in this alone. If you are in your twenties, you are not the first one who was tempted to leave the old paths and the old standards.

If you are in your thirties, you are not the first person tempted to discouragement and depression because of your disappointment in yourself and others.

If you are in your forties, you are not the first woman to say, "Enough is enough already. Where do I go to retire early?"

If you are over 43, I do not understand your temptation, but I imagine someday I will. Until then, I can say, "I love you," and I can remind you that God is with you. The older I get, the greater my temptations seem and the more sufficient and com-

forting seems the presence of God.

Let me also begin this section by saying that you are not necessarily being tempted because you are a terrible Christian, nor are you tempted because you are particularly weak or crazy. Perhaps, you are a Spirit-filled lady who has been led into temptation, so that you might help others better in your own Promised Land which God has prepared for your future.

May I also say that it is possible to come out of your temptation as a Spirit-filled Christian with no major regrets. Luke 4:14 says, *"And Jesus returned in the power of the Spirit..."* This is describing the way that Jesus came out of His wilderness experience.

Lastly, if you are not presently feeling tempted, future temptations will come. Luke 4:13 says, *"And when the devil had ended all the temptation, he departed from him for a season."*

It is my desire in the next three chapters to encourage those who are enduring a season of temptation, and to prepare those who are not, for the temptations which lie ahead. I trust these insights will be of help to you.

Meeting Your Needs Your Way

When Dr. Schaap and I had been married for four and one-half years, I told him I wanted to look for a new house. At the time, a lot of my high school friends were becoming successful in business and buying beautiful, large houses. "Cindy," he replied, "We have not gone after material things in our marriage, and we are not going to start now. If God wants us to have a new house, He will have to show us."

I remember very clearly my conversation with God which occurred later on that same day. I was ironing when I prayed, "Dear Lord, my husband is right; we will not seek material things in our marriage. We will live where we are unless You clearly show us that Your will is otherwise." I also remember feeling a lot of security as I reflected upon the values of the husband God had given me. However, that was not the first time, and it has not been the last time that I have been tempted to get things my way.

The Devil came to Jesus during His season of temptation and said, *"If thou be the Son of God, command this stone that it be made bread."* Jesus had fasted 40 days, and He was hungry. The Devil knew his weakest point, and the Devil tempted Jesus to try to get what He wanted in some other way than the Father's way.

This is a common temptation which many women face. *"There hath no temptation taken you but such as is common to man...."* We women often try to get things our own way by doing the following:

1. Dating or marrying whom we choose instead of who

God chooses, maybe because we are feeling desperate.

2. Choosing a college, secular or Christian, based upon what will get us the best paying job.

3. Starting a career in order to make more money, even though it is against the will of God or the will of our husband.

4. Spending extra time at work, even though it causes us to slack in the training of our children.

5. Nagging our husbands or conniving a way to get a bigger house, a better car, or whatever we want or think we need.

6. Charging items that we know we cannot afford on a credit card. Ouch!

7. Scheming ways to be asked to fill positions or get opportunities which God could give us in His own way and time.

The list could go on and on. Do any of them sound personally familiar? They do to me, and I am sure they do to you also. Our temptations are common. It is when we try to convince ourselves and others that our temptation is not common that we get ourselves into trouble. Our temptation is as old as the Devil.

And the answer is as reliable as the Bible. How did Jesus respond to the Devil when he tempted Jesus to get things apart from God's will? He reminded the Devil that the Word of God was the most important as He replied, "*...It is written, Man shall not live by bread alone, but by every word that proceedeth out of the mouth of God.*" (Matthew 4:4)

Jesus used the Word of God to help Him to make His decisions during His season of temptation. So, I have found the Bible to be the answer in my times of temptation. That is why I have memorized it, read it, and studied it. Sometimes the answer was obvious; I just needed to quit making myself an exception. Other times the answer was slow in coming, but the answer always came. The Word of God has always been sufficient.

Shortly after Brother Schaap's and my decision about a house, God gave us the house of our dreams. I placed a plaque bearing the verse, Matthew 6:33, *"But seek ye first the kingdom of God, and his righteousness; and all these things shall be added unto you."* upon the mantel above our fireplace.

One evening a few years later, I turned off the living room lights before I went to bed. I passed the living room a few minutes later, and I discovered that I had accidentally left on a spotlight above our fireplace mantel. The light was shining on Matthew 6:33. I looked at the picture of my husband and me to the left of the light and at the picture of my son which was further left. I glanced over at the picture of my daughter to the right. Then I viewed all of the signs of God's blessings which were located in just one room of our house—our living room. I felt the peace of knowing that none of these things had been obtained by leaving God's will. I thought of some others I knew who had since strayed from church and perhaps even lost their families while seeking material things. My heart grieved for them; yet, my heart also rejoiced as my eyes returned to the words of Matthew 6:33, *"But seek ye first the kingdom of God...and all these things shall be added unto you."*

"Dear Lord," I prayed, "You really did come through, didn't You? Good night, my Father. I know that my sleep in You shall be peaceful. I'll talk to You in the morning."

Ladies, during each day and through each decade of your life, resist the common temptation to meet your own needs (and desires) in your own way. The Devil really, really is a liar. His way (or your own way) is not best. Through each year and each decade that passes, you will see that God really does come through.

Proving Ourselves

In Luke 4:9, the Devil tempted Jesus to cast Himself down off the pinnacle of the temple in order that Jesus might prove that He is the Son of God.

Jesus responded with the words in Luke 4:12, "...*It is said, Thou shalt not tempt the Lord thy God.*" Jesus recognized that the desire to prove Himself to the Devil was a temptation which should be resisted through the use of God's Word.

If we looked behind many of the bad decisions which we as women make, I think we would see that they began with the temptation to prove ourselves.

The strong-willed child is often merely trying to prove that he can act independently of his parents.

Teenage girls are tempted to prove themselves. I am often introduced around the country to "the best soul winner and the best girl in the youth group." When I ask that girl what she is going to do with her life after high school, she may respond, "I am going to 'such-and-such university' and study law." I look in her eyes and seem to see the look of a girl who is trying to prove herself.

Young and middle-aged married ladies sometimes leave the job of housekeeping to pursue a career or to start the business they have always wanted. I wonder if the overextending of themselves (which usually leads to the breakdown of the family) may have started with a temptation for these ladies to prove themselves.

Please don't misunderstand me. I am not judging every woman to be wrong who attends a certain college, pursues a certain degree, or follows a certain career. Though I write and teach principles that have helped me and are aimed at helping other Christian women, I do not allow myself to judge the lifestyles of others. I do not judge whether or not you should be doing what you are doing. I do not know what is right for you and would not try to determine that.

However, I know that time and time again in my own life, the Devil has tempted me to prove myself. At times in my life, I have seen other women accomplish certain tasks, and thought to myself, "I could do that." Fortunately, through God's Word, I have learned that this desire—to prove I could do it—is not a good criteria for making decisions or planning a life.

Instead, I need to recognize that this desire could be a temptation from the Devil, and I need to use God's Word to guide my life. Allow me to illustrate. When my children were small, I spent most of my time at home. After Jaclynn started school, I was left at home to take care of our son Kenny. Much of life revolved around playing with one little boy. I did this to open Kenny's heart to me, so that he might be willing to listen to my training. I did this because I thought it was what God and my husband wanted me to do.

When Kenny was about four years old, I played baseball with him for a half an hour or so every afternoon. If you had looked for me at this time, you would have actually found me running bases around our side yard. I guess I must have given the neighbors something to talk about at the dinner table.

I enjoyed my time with Kenny, but there were days when I wondered if I was doing the right thing. I would ask myself questions such as:

- "Am I lazy?"
- "Did I get a college degree for this?"
- "Is life passing right by me?"

And when I heard of other ladies' accomplishments, my pride sometimes responded with a silent, "I could do that."

Each morning I opened the Bible for my time with the Lord. It was then when I heard a voice saying, "You are doing the right thing." I am not saying that this is right for every woman. I am saying that it was the right thing for me to resist the temptation to prove myself and to follow what God's Word showed me to do.

I believe this is what the Bible means when it says, *"For my yoke is easy, and my burden is light."* (Matthew 11:30) When we are working for the Lord, we do not have the burden of proving ourselves to people. I have found that the Lord is easier to please in some ways than people are.

I remember one morning reading Psalm 37:7a which says, *"Rest in the LORD, and wait patiently for him: fret not thyself because of him who prospereth in his way."* This verse became very special to me during this stage of my life.

I also found a definition for slothfulness which helped me during this time. Slothfulness is doing anything other than what God wants you to do at any given moment. If I am doing what God wants me to do, I can rest in Him, even if the rest of the world may not understand my priorities.

So, dear reader, I am not trying to set your priorities or plan your life for you. I am only suggesting that you not plan your life according to your desire to prove yourself. Instead, recognize this desire as the temptation that it is. Plan your life to please your husband and according to God's Word.

The other day Kenny and I were alone in the car together. "Mom," Kenny asked, "Do you remember that when I was a little boy, you read a book or took a walk with me every afternoon? You let me choose which one I wanted to do?"

"Yes, Kenny, I remember. Do you remember that I used to play baseball with you each afternoon? It's probably because of me that you're a good athlete," I responded facetiously.

"I remember, Mom, but I am not an athlete because of you. You were a lousy pitcher."

"Mom," Kenny continued, "do you remember all of the Nerf sports we played in our house during the winter? We must have played every Nerf sport there was."

"Yes, Kenny," I replied. "It's amazing that our house is still in one piece. I am glad you remember."

"I do, Mom," Kenny finished. "I remember."

My time spent with Kenny will not be listed in the *Guinness Book of World Records*. (My pitching could be listed in Ripley's Believe It or Not!) I wasn't impressing anyone, not even myself, when I spent time with one little boy. But I was doing something important. I was doing something that I am afraid Christian women have forgotten to make important. I was doing what I knew God wanted me to do at that time of my life.

And when Kenny said, "Mom, I remember," I felt very important. I felt no regret. I felt relieved that I had not listened to the Devil or to my own ugly pride. I felt that I had nothing to prove.

May we all continue to strive to do at each moment exactly what the Word of God would have us to do.

The Desire for Position

Some time ago, I did a study on the temptations of Jesus. I found many truths that helped me personally and that I felt would be a help to women of all ages. I decided to share those truths in the *Christian Womanhood* paper.

At that time, I had no idea that I would be writing the final article in the series as the wife of the pastor of First Baptist Church of Hammond, Indiana. It seemed a little ironic that this article was about the desire for position.

The Devil took Jesus *"up into an exceeding high mountain...."* (Matthew 4:8) The Devil promised to give Jesus *"all the kingdoms of the world, and the glory of them"* if Jesus would fall down and worship the Devil.

Jesus responded by quoting the Bible, *"...for it is written, Thou shalt worship the Lord thy God, and him only shalt thou serve."* I believe if we examined the many temptations that women of all ages face today, we would find many of them stemming from the desire for position or for popularity.

Children and teenage girls submit to peer pressure and do things they know are wrong. Why? To hold a position of high esteem among their peers.

Adult women follow dreams that do not run parallel with God's purpose for their lives. Why? So they can brag to others and feel good about themselves or about obtaining some lofty position. Titles like doctor, lawyer, accountant, professor, or even secretary are often considered to the world to be acceptable and, perhaps, impressive. On the other hand, titles like wife, homemaker, mother, or even grandmother are scorned more and more by society. I must admit that when asked to write my profession on bank applications and so forth, I have written teacher or professor instead of homemaker. Yet the truth is I have spent most of my life being a wife, mother, and homemaker.

When people ask me my profession and I share with them that I am a college teacher, they seem impressed. When local people ask me where I teach, I answer Hyles-Anderson College; and they now seem unimpressed. I once chuckled to myself that just once I would like to tell them that I teach law at Harvard. All of us humans share a desire to impress others with our position.

But there is one problem—this desire has nothing to do with why we were made. We were made to worship and to serve God. When the Devil tempted Jesus with position, Jesus used the Bible to put this desire into perspective and reminded the Devil that Jesus was made to glorify the Father.

Though faced with the same temptations as other women, I have strived to resist desiring position. I have instead strived to do in my life what I felt would please God according to the purpose He has for me. Since 1979, I have felt that my purpose was to glorify God and to help my husband, Jack Schaap, do what God made him to do.

Does that mean I have desired position for my husband? No, it does not! I have only wanted my husband to serve God in the way God has planned for him. Since 1979, I have prayed daily that Brother Schaap would do in his life what God made him to do. And I have frequently told my husband that I didn't care what that was. I have told him that if God made him to shine the shoes of the other men on the staff here at our church, I would be proud. I only want him to do what God has planned for him, and I want him to glorify God.

I have always believed my husband to be a great Christian.

Yet I know that the greatest task he can do in life is that for which God made him. Shining shoes in God's will can be used in a greater way than pastoring out of God's will. *And I also know how devilish a woman can become when she desires position for her husband.*

For years, I have prayed that God would choose the right leader to perpetuate my father's ministry to be what it ought to be for the next generation. I never prayed that person would be my husband. I only prayed that God would use my husband greatly, doing what God made him to do, and that Brother Schaap would glorify God.

It is the Devil who causes us to desire position, and the Devil's chief tactic is to sow strife among the brethren. I have not wished to desire position because I feared that desiring such would hinder me from loving my brothers and sisters in Christ.

Am I pleased with my husband's perpetuating the ministry of my father? Yes, I am pleased and honored that God has chosen him. God has answered my prayer of many decades in great and mighty ways which I knew not.

Yet when I reach Heaven, I do not think God will be terribly impressed with my title as pastor's wife of First Baptist Church of Hammond, Indiana. I think God will be pleased if I have won souls and helped people. I think God will be pleased if I have encouraged a man of God. In fact, "Man of God Encourager" sounds like an impressive title to me.

When I was a little girl, I used to go by my daddy's office. I especially loved to go by after my dad had preached an unusually hard sermon. I learned to watch for a vulnerable look on his face, and I learned to be especially positive when I saw that look.

"Dad," I would say when I saw that vulnerable look, "I'm proud of you for preaching so hard."

"Cindy," he would respond with a grin, "You love it when I'm mean. The meaner I preach, the more you like it. Thank you for stopping by."

I watched the vulnerable look turn into a confident one, and I would leave the office and go on my way. I would feel I had done my small part to encourage the man of God. There is no title or position for such a job, but it is the one in which I have found the most fulfillment in my life.

Now I go to the same office and sometimes see the same vulnerable look. I encourage a new man of God. My feeling is one of loneliness for the man who once stood there and pride in the one who stands there now. Most of all my feeling is one of fulfillment for I am doing what I know I do best—what I believe I was made to do.

I am honored to be a pastor's wife. But call me something else instead. Call me a "Man of God Encourager." I know anyone can do it. I know it's not really a title or a position, but God doesn't need a title or position to do great things through us. He can do great things through the simple words we speak and deeds we do for which there is no title. And He can do those things through anyone who wants to serve Him and who believes in Him.

So let's not think about position as we plan our lives and pray for our husbands. Let's just think about serving and worshiping God and what if...well, maybe it seems too ridiculous, but what if...perhaps I'm being a bit too trite...yet, what if...maybe I just don't understand today's society or fundamental politics, but what if...we really were made just to glorify God?

Walking with God
on the
Bright Side

Build Up Yourself

I have always disliked hearing someone speak too highly of himself. I have heard that you dislike in others what you fight in yourself, so maybe I am revealing a weakness rather than a strength when I admit this.

I enjoy hearing the accomplishments of others when they are helpful, but I have a difficult time hearing someone take his own goodness too seriously. I am as guilty as anyone of wanting to have my good deeds noticed. But I do try to remember the words in Proverbs 27:2 which say, *"Let another man praise thee, and not thine own mouth; a stranger, and not thine own lips."* So, it is unique for me to write something on building up yourself. Yet, that is exactly what I am saying! It is time for us, as fundamental Christian wives and mothers, to build ourselves. It is time to forget about building our husbands, our children, and others. It is time to build number one—ourselves! (As you can see, I have really become a woman of the nineties—oops! I mean a woman of the new millennium!)

Actually, I am as old-fashioned as ever. It's just that I was reading my Bible the other day and came across Jude 20. *"But ye, beloved, building up yourselves on your most holy faith, praying in the Holy Ghost."*

Several years ago, I started a Bible study on the subject of faith and fear. From that Bible study, I wrote several articles for *Christian Womanhood*. For two years, I built my faith; and I learned things that will help me to build my faith for the rest of my life. The result has been more than and different than I expected. The next verse, Jude 21, will explain: *"Keep your-*

selves in the love of God, looking for the mercy of our Lord Jesus Christ unto eternal life."

As my faith was being built, I also found that my love was strengthened. Not only did I find that I loved my husband and children more, I also found more love for those who don't necessarily love me and mine. You see, if someone attacks me, my husband, or someone else whom I love, my faith tells me God has allowed this to happen for our good and that God will take care of it. My part is to do what Jude 20 says and build my faith while "...*praying in the Holy Ghost.*" Prayer and walking with the Holy Spirit are the bridges that build my faith and keep me in the love of God.

When I turned 40, I did not dread it at all. My husband and my children made me feel tremendously honored at this time in my life. Though I did not dread turning 40, I must admit that I am not always impressed with my age group. Middle-aged people like I am often criticize children and teenagers because they are so mean to each other. We also criticize older people because they are sometimes "old and crabby." But, if they are not careful, middle-aged people can be the meanest and crabbiest of all. Why?

We are suddenly realizing how fast time flies. Soon we will be old. We are uncertain how many years we have left to make our mark on the world, and we may find ourselves disappointed with what little we have accomplished so far. Add to that the stress of rearing teenagers and hoping our kids turn out as good as our neighbors, and, if we are not careful, middle-aged people can be the meanest of all—stepping on whoever gets in our way.

What is the answer? I believe the answer is to look out for number one and build ourselves. That is, we should build our own faith. My faith tells me that God will use me in the way that is best for me. Therefore, I can love those who may seem to be used in a way I would have chosen for myself. My faith tells me that God will have a place for me in the future; so I can love those with whom I might have felt tempted to jockey for position. My faith tells me that God will use my children in the way that is best for them. So guess what? I can love my neighbor's children, even if they got the award that my children wanted.

Do you understand what I am saying? The building of my own faith keeps me loving others with the love of God. It is interesting to me that these verses close a book that is mainly about *hating* false doctrine. I am not for loving the doctrine of those who are against the faith of the Bible, nor am I for socializing with backslidden and worldly Christians. I am strongly opposed to that.

Yet, I am just as strong for loving my fellow workers in the service of God, and I am strong for loving my enemies—because God commands me to. If you have ever had someone hate you or hate someone you love, and if you have looked in your heart to find not hatred, but love and forgiveness, you have experienced a Red-Sea-type miracle. This is worth experiencing over and over.

Why do middle-aged people like myself get mean and crabby? It is because we are trying to use the time that we have to make a difference. Often, we are trying to make a good difference. We forget though that it is God Who makes the difference and not ourselves. My faith tells me that we can trust Him. And my faith tells me that I can love you.

How then will I make a difference with my life? Oh, God covers that too, in the next verse, Jude 22: "*And of some have compassion, making a difference.*" Jude 23 follows and is a wonderful verse about winning souls and changing lives. Yes, the goal is to win souls and change lives, not just love, love, love everyone. But first, I must build my faith; secondly, my faith will keep me in the love of God; then, compassion will follow. And, oh, what a difference compassion makes.

With the Holy Spirit and compassion, we can win souls, see lives changed, and truly make a difference; and, in so doing, we won't have to step on our fellow workers. Instead, perhaps, we can make a difference in their lives, too.

And so ladies—it is our turn! Forget about building your husband, your children, or anyone else. Think about old number one. Think about yourself and build yourself. I challenge you to build your own faith, that is. And then hold on. You are going to find yourself loving like you have never before loved…and God is going to make the difference!

Learning to Love

I had memorized much of the New Testament, and I had never told a soul. My family was aware of my memorization program that had been going on for several years, but they had no idea how much I had accomplished. It was, to me, a very personal matter which I did not feel comfortable advertising even to those closest to me. Yet, I had come to an impasse in my spiritual life, and I was surprised and frustrated at how much I was failing in this one area of my Christian walk.

My husband and I both read the Bible near each other every morning about 5:00 A.M. On one of those mornings, I sat in the living room easy chair feeling confused and disappointed in myself. In exasperation, I proclaimed to my husband, "I have memorized most of the New Testament…" Brother Schaap looked both serious and surprised. "…and I'm still not a very good Christian!" Brother Schaap looked amused, and we both began laughing. My frustration with how much I yet needed to grow in my Christian life had caused me to let the cat out of the bag. My secret was no longer a secret.

Not only did I talk with my husband about this seeming impasse in my Christian life, but I also talked to God.

God, how can a person like myself absorb so much of Your Word, try so hard to be a good Christian, and still be such a lousy one in this particular area in which I am struggling? Please show me the way!

During my early morning devotions at that time, I was reviewing a book of the Bible I had already memorized. That book was I Corinthians. One morning it became time to review chapter 13 of I Corinthians. As I read these verses, I seemed to understand why I was so exasperated. God, in His mercy, answered my earlier prayer, and He began to show me the way.

I read verses 1 and 2: *"Though I speak with the tongues of men and of angels, and have not charity, I am become as sounding brass, or a tinkling cymbal. And though I have the gift of prophecy, and understand all mysteries, and all knowledge; and though I have all faith, so that I could remove mountains, and have not charity, I am nothing."*

I soon came to verse 8, *"Charity never faileth: but whether there be prophecies, they shall fail; whether there be tongues, they shall cease; whether there be knowledge, it shall vanish away."*

I proceeded to verse 13, *"And now abideth faith, hope, charity, these three; but the greatest of these is charity."* There I found why I was struggling with my particular problem. I had not yet learned to love as I should. My knowledge of the Bible could only take me so far in my Christian life. But I now faced some things that could only be conquered with God's most powerful tool. That tool is love.

My father was sometimes criticized for trying to help pastors who had fallen into sin. Though he had never recommended a man to return to the pastorate after that man had fallen morally, my dad did all he could to help rebuild the fallen man's life. Sometimes he would work to rebuild a man with whom other preachers would not even communicate. Usually those who rebuked him for doing so were younger preachers. In my opinion, they were Christians who had obtained their B.S. degree in knowledge but who had not gone on to receive their doctorate in charity.

I am afraid that I am often more like those younger critics than I am like my dear daddy. I have strived to learn my Bible. My knowledge of the Bible has left me with a hatred for sin and a love for righteousness. Though I am far from attaining it, the word *holiness* is one of my favorite words. You see, to me, everything is black or white. Yet, at the time I was reviewing I Corinthians 13, it seemed to me that God was saying, "Cindy, you are struggling in this area of your Christian life because you have not graduated yet. While trying to obtain your Master's degree in knowledge, you have not yet entered the kindergarten class in love."

It is not that my knowledge of the Bible has let me down. I have enjoyed and profited from each moment spent in God's Word. In fact, it was my memorization of the Bible that led me to the answer to my problem. But my knowledge of the Bible is not enough in itself to make me a good Christian. I need faith, I need hope, and what I need most is love.

Dear reader, do you find yourself at an impasse in your Christian life? In your marriage? Or in your child rearing? Do you find yourself unable to forgive a friend? Do you wonder why your time spent in the Bible and in prayer still seems to leave you far short of being like Jesus? Perhaps your problem is like mine—you need to give more of yourself to learning to love like Jesus did.

I used to somewhat sneer in my mind at the wife who stayed with her husband though he failed her time after time morally. Doesn't a wife enable her husband to do wrong when she stays with him while he repeatedly fails her? Doesn't this wife realize that she has biblical grounds for divorce?

I was convicted when I again read these words, *"And now abideth faith, hope, charity, these three; but the greatest of these is charity."*

Perhaps God sees the betrayed, yet loyal, wife as the greatest Christian of all. You see, she has no reason for faith. She has no reason to trust her husband to be faithful to her as I do to trust mine. She has no hope. There is no evidence to prove to her that things will get better in the future. She stays with her husband solely because she loves him. I wonder if my Bible memorization pales in comparison to the Ph.D. the betrayed wife has earned in God's favorite subject—love.

This chapter, however, is not about divorce or betrayal. It is about all of the ways we still struggle with our lives and relationships in spite of all the things that we have learned. This chapter is about taking the next step in our Christian lives and learning to love as Christ did.

Dear Lord, Teach me to love. Amen.

What I Am Learning About Love

When I was in high school, I was extremely outgoing. Perhaps you would even call me the "leader type." During my senior year, our school newspaper printed predictions about what each senior student would be doing in ten years. It was predicted that I would be pastoring a church with 10,000 members, and my husband would be the piano player. And then I met Jack Schaap...

It's amazing what love will do to you sometimes. I recognized in my husband-to-be an extreme amount of leadership potential. I felt God wanted to use him, and that it was God's will that I be Brother Schaap's helpmeet. I purposely placed myself in the shadows and even quieted my personality quite a bit, believing that I might hinder my husband if I did not. I have felt quite comfortable, and I have even reveled in my quieter position.

In 1996 my husband was asked to fill the role of vice president at Hyles-Anderson College. After accepting, Brother Schaap came to me with a request. "Cindy, I want you to become a lot more involved in the college. I want you to be more visible, maybe even more outgoing, like you were in high school." Being the submissive wife that I am, I bristled.

You see, I don't like change, and I could not quite understand why my husband felt he needed me to be something different when I had tried so hard to be the opposite just for him.

Please don't get me wrong...my husband has always made me feel loved and completely accepted. I have never felt less than desirable when being held against his magnifying glass of approval. I believe my husband realized that if our marriage was to maintain its closeness during this significant change in our lives, we both were going to have to make some adjustments. I thought all of this through and being the submissive wife that I am...I still bristled. "Though I love the college," I reasoned, "I am busy writing a book and do not have time to take on any new responsibilities."

God understood that He had some work to do in my life. Once again as I was reviewing I Corinthians 13, I decided to do some studying. I came to the phrase that says, *"beareth all things."* I looked up the word *beareth* in my New Testament dictionary, and I found the following definition: *to take upon one-self or to bear up under.*

The Holy Spirit spoke to my heart. He seemed to say, "Cindy, when you truly love someone, you take up anything he asks you to take up; you bear up under any load. You are willing to endure what he asks you to endure or to become what he asks you to become."

It has been over 25 years since I started dating Jack Schaap. In the ensuing years, his needs have changed significantly. He does not need the exact same type of wife that he did almost 25 years ago when I became his bride. Why? Because he is not exactly the same person that he was in 1979 as a new groom.

This may seem a bit paradoxical, but the ability of a marriage to stay as fresh and exciting as it was in its youth is determined to a great degree upon the willingness of its partners to change. We must change according to the ever-changing needs of the ones we love. Over 25 years ago, I began dating a 19-year-old boy. Now, through I am married to someone with the same name, he is not the same person. He is now a 45-year-old man. If I love him, I will be willing to change as the needs of my husband change.

"Okay, Holy Spirit," I said that morning as I closed my New Testament dictionary and my Bible, "I am starting to get the point. No more bristling for me...at least, I'll do my best. Whatever my husband needs me to be or do, that is what I'll do." I walked away confidently, but found myself upon my knees once more not too much later.

Dear Lord,

May I please ask You a favor? Would You come and be exactly what my husband needs through me? Together we can make any needed adjustments just fine...

...And that, dear reader, is what I'm learning about love.

Like a Sister

"Say unto wisdom, Thou art my sister; and call understanding thy kinswoman." (Proverbs 7:4)

I have two sisters with whom I have always enjoyed a close and meaningful relationship. My sisters, Becky and Linda, live about 1,000 miles away from me in Plano, Texas, which is a suburb of Dallas. Occasionally, one of them comes to Indiana for a visit. I always look forward to these visits with great joy. I usually mark my calendar in bold print with the words "Linda is coming!" or "Becky will be here!" When I come to the part of my calendar that records the day they will be leaving, I feel a little bit of sadness even though my sisters have not even arrived yet.

When my sisters come to visit, we stay up late at night talking. I believe we do this because we can't stand to see one day of our visit come to a close. We get up early in the morning so we can begin our visiting as soon as possible. We fix our hair, put on our makeup, etc., at the same time so that we won't miss a minute of conversation.

I consider myself a woman of priority. I struggle to put my relationships in proper order and believe that my husband should come first amongst my earthly relationships. However, he would tell you that I have difficulty remembering my priorities when my sisters come to visit.

Linda, Becky, and I do not consider ourselves to have had a good visit unless we have literally laughed until we cried. When we are together, we reminisce of childhood days. We laugh about things that would not even interest anyone else. We find ourselves saying to each other, "You think just like I do," or "We both are just like mom in that way." We ask each other, "Do you do that too?" and we say, "I thought I was the only one who did that." My sisters and I understand each other very well.

I have been especially close to my sister Linda. In fact, I have always adored her. She is so many things that I would like to be. She is tall and blonde, while I am short and brunette. She is musically talented and artistically creative, where I am not. She is poised, while I am mischievous.

While we were growing up in our parents' home, Linda always took my dad's advice and made him feel ten feet tall for giving it. I was more prone to argue before taking his advice. Linda laughed hysterically at my dad's jokes and made him feel like a real comedian; in a monotone voice I said, "That's funny, Dad."

Linda was scared of spiders, and my dad killed many of them for her. She always made Dad feel like he had caught a grizzly bear. I told them both that they were being ridiculous. Linda gave me badly-needed advice about how to dress, how much makeup to wear, and how to behave. She was always there when I needed her.

Several years ago, Linda moved 1,000 miles away. (She had previously lived around the corner from my home.) Our visits together have been few and far between since then. Also since then, my sister Becky came down with a serious illness which makes it increasingly more difficult to spend time together.

Baby sisters are notorious for giving advice to their older sisters. I am a baby sister, and I played the part very well. I told my older sisters how to be good wives and mothers before I was married and had children of my own. It is amazing that they let me live to tell about it. I was very much a know-it-all. As I have grown older, I have often called my sisters to ask for their advice. I have asked them for advice about child rearing, housekeeping, recipes, etc. They have always been available, and they have had the answers for which I was looking.

During the long absences of my dear sisters, I have made a new friend. I have made friends with the wisdom which is found in God's Word. This friend has never left my side. It has remained on the nightstand beside my bed, in my purse, in my car, and in the attaché which I carry when I am going to teach. I don't mark it on my calendar, but I look forward to my meeting with the Bible with great anticipation. I often laugh and cry while I read its words. I find myself sad to see our time together end, and I wonder how long I will be able to make it without spending time in it. I have discovered that the Author of the Word of God understands me better than I understand myself. I sometimes get up early and stay up late to skim its pages. I find myself wanting to have it with me in everything I do.

As we have grown older, our questions have become far more complex. I find myself often saying to my sisters, "I don't know the answer. All I can say is to seek the Lord on the matter." It is wonderful to know that my new friend, the Bible, can be there for my sisters and me when we cannot be there for each other.

Every human being alive has questions which can only be answered by seeking the wisdom of God's Word. That is why God commands us to love the wisdom of His Word like a sister. Perhaps you do not have a sister, and you do not relate to the passage of Scripture in Proverbs 7:4. I imagine you do have some "kinswoman," a close friend or relative with whom you have sweet memories like the ones I have described above. God commands us to love the Bible like we love that special lady who is like a sister to us. Please allow me to share with you some ways to increase your love for the Bible.

1. Read it. I generally read two chapters from both Testaments and a Psalm and a Proverb every day. I have my devotions during the best time of my day.

2. Memorize it. I started memorizing the Bible daily several years ago. During the last few years, I have begun memorizing entire chapters and books. I put it off for several years because I thought it would be too hard, but I finally gave in to the Lord. My Bible memory has been such a blessing to me.

A couple of practical tips about Bible memory that have helped me are as follows:

• Keep a record of what you have memorized in the back of your Bible. That way you will be less prone to lose them. You will also have a record so that your children may have a glimpse of your Bible memory program when you have gone to Heaven.

• Memorize two new verses of the chapter you are working on each day and then go over the verses you have previously learned. Also, review another previously learned passage. I review previously learned passages two verses at a time daily until I have reviewed the entire chapter.

3. Study it. I have found it difficult to study the Bible each day. It works best for me to schedule one hour or so a week when I study my Bible. Do something you enjoy to help you study the Bible. I enjoy working on my word processor of my computer. When I study the Bible, I read a passage about a particular person or theme I am studying. I then type on my computer all the facts I wish to remember about that topic. I then type all the things about those facts which I can apply to my own life. Sometimes I use a commentary. More often than not I use only my Bible and my brain. Two good ideas would be to study the life of Jesus and the lives of the ladies in the Bible. Another good idea would be to write in a journal for Bible study.

4. Meditate on it. I have found since I have started memorizing and studying the Bible, I have no trouble remembering to meditate on it. The verses which have become so imprinted on my mind and my heart seem to minister to me and the particular need I am having each day.

5. Teach it. It is sometimes difficult for me to teach the Bible through writing and speaking because the lives of our family have been so much of an open book already. However, I find as I share God's Word through teaching and soul winning, it becomes even more like a sister to me.

I am thankful that God puts verses in the Bible which relate so aptly to our innermost feelings. Surely He had me in mind when He said to call wisdom your sister.

"I thank You, Lord, that You understand what I mean when I say, 'I love you and I love the wisdom of Your Word—like a sister.' "

When God Is Enough

During a rough time in my dad's ministry, my dad often said to me (with a little bit of exasperation) that I needed to learn that God could run the world without my help. Unfortunately, of the four children in our family, I believe that I am the slowest learner. I have a knack of learning things the hard way. If there is anything that I learned during that time (or shall I say began to learn), it's that God really is enough when it comes to handling problems in our lives and in the lives of those we love. Please allow me to share some areas where I am learning that only God is enough.

1. God is enough to be our confidanté. At times friends have asked me how I or my family were doing. I sensed the concern in their faces and wanted to share with them how we really were doing, but I opened my mouth and the word "fine" came out. I have often walked away and wished that I could have shared myself with them. I knew that they would have felt closer to me and I to them if I could have shared with them more. However, any of us who have been around any length of time at all know that there are some things we simply cannot share nor would be wise to share with others.

I am thankful for the confidantés with whom I have been able to share throughout my life. I am thankful for a husband who is long on patience and godly advice. I am also thankful to my family for being there for me in ways that no one else could understand. However, I did learn during that time that God is really enough to be our confidanté. It was during that time that I began to walk two miles every morning. I didn't begin this for spiritual reasons, but rather because I had been eating too much ice cream and needed the exercise.

The Lord, though, had other things in mind. I began to use these walks to tell the Lord how I was really doing. I am so thankful for the verse, Psalm 142:2, which says, "*I poured out my complaint before him; I shewed before him my trouble.*" Sometimes I don't feel like saying, "I'm fine." Instead, I feel like saying, "I'm just plain mad," or "I can't believe how hurt I feel." Maybe you like to complain, too. Somehow we housewives don't mind doing the work as long as we can complain a bit in the process. Our complaining, though, will be spiritually damaging to those around us.

How wonderful to know that we can go to God and tell Him how we really feel and to know that He'll be none the weaker! The closeness that we feel with Him at these times is so special, and so often during hard times I've prayed and asked the Lord to help that concerned person to feel my love, even though there were many things I could not share with them.

2. God is enough to defend us. Anyone who accomplishes anything in life is going to be the object of criticism. At times it seems that there are two groups of people in the Lord's work—those who serve Him and those who critique those who serve Him. If God's servants spend their time defending themselves, they will have little time to be doing anything fruitful for Him.

Psalm 62:2 tells us that God is our defense. There are many verses in the Bible that speak of God defending us. I read these verses several times before I realized that they applied to me. I thought they only applied to those who fought in real battles, and I knew I would never be a soldier in a real battle like King David was. However, as time passes, I realize that life is a spiritual battle and that I need God to defend me. I need to ask Him to defend when I or someone I love is criticized, and I need to believe that He will. I also need to trust Him to defend me when I have said or done something that I should not have.

Sometimes, when I am speaking publicly, I may say something that I realize later I should not have said. I always pray that I will have discretion in my speech and will not say anything that I should not. Because I am human, I still say things that were not best. I often pray that the Lord will defend what was said or help the listeners to understand what I meant. We cannot do anything much for the Lord until we can come to the place that we give our best and then trust the Holy Spirit to defend us and to do what we cannot do.

3. God is enough to right injustice. I must admit that there are times when things do not seem fair to me. I may feel tempted to go tell someone off or to give my opinion as to how a certain situation should have been handled. It is sometimes the right thing for us to handle a situation Biblically if we are in a position to do so. Sometimes, I am tempted to handle or give advice about a situation that I know is none of my business. At times like this the Lord reminds me of verses like *"He that passeth by, and meddleth with strife belonging not to him, is like one that taketh a dog by the ears."* (Proverbs 26:17) *"And withal they learn to be idle, wandering about from house to house; and not only idle, but tattlers also and busybodies, speaking things which they ought not."* (I Timothy 5:13)

I often wonder if my children will really learn to trust the Lord if I tell them to do so, yet at the same time run here and there trying to solve other people's problems. If I have begun to learn anything in the past year, it is the Lord begins to work best when I give in and decide to do nothing but pray. God simply waits for us to realize that He really is enough.

I am beginning to understand that the only things that can stop the work of the devil are the prayers of the saints. The devil uses gossip, worry, and meddling to stop our prayers. In our own power, we are powerless.

4. God is enough to keep us close to Him. If there is anything that I have been grateful for it is that God has kept me in His perfect will despite trials and temptations. A lot of that is due to the fine leadership in my life, but even more is due to God Himself. Very little has to do with me.

The Christian life was so much of a struggle as I prayed that God would help me to do this and that. My prayer so much more has been, "God, You do all of the work. Please reach out and pull me close to Yourself, especially when I don't want to be close to You." I always want to want to be close to Him, but I don't always want to like I should. How comforting to realize that God only expects me to do my part in staying close to Him! That is to *"pray without ceasing"* and then to lean on Him to do the rest.

Perhaps you are getting the idea that I am simply saying what we've all heard before. That is that God is enough for anything. I must confess that I am one of those people who collects lists of instructions for success. For example, I have many lists that tell me "Secrets to Child Rearing." I feel the Lord is pleased when we do what we can in rearing our children, but I often wonder if He is not just looking for parents who will just simply lean on Him in every area of their lives. What better example could there be for our children?

There are days when I wonder what the future might hold for Christianity as the coming of our Lord seems to be approaching. I must confess that sometimes I worry a little. (My dad told me not to worry also.) However, my worries are put aside once more when I remember the testimony of those like Paul who found that God was enough even in a prison cell.

I'm thankful for the trials of our lives. They teach us lessons that can apply to every area of our lives, even our uncertain future. So you see, I am finally learning what my dad had so patiently tried to teach me all these years. God can run this world without my help (or yours, for that matter) and whatever the future holds God certainly will forever be enough to cause me to live on the bright side of eternity.

From the Publisher

"*Revolutionary!*" That was my wife's answer to the question I had posed to her.

The question was this: "What do you think about the manuscript for Mrs. Schaap's new book?"

So from that moment, we at Christian Womanhood set about to try to "make it happen" and publish this book.

My wife has a close walk with God and a keen understanding of the needs of Christian women. So when she said the ideas in this book were revolutionary after reading it, I had to do what I could do get it published.

Cindy Schaap is a proven author, a gifted speaker, and a committed Christian.

I have known her for over 20 years and have seen her and her husband consistently live on the bright side. They have exhibited what Brother Schaap refers to as "bone-deep" joy. As you read these pages, you will be blessed, convicted, and helped by the revolutionary principles taught within its pages. Enjoy!

– Dan Wolfe
Managing Editor